I0481178

Happy Halloween
Coloring Fun for the Whole Family

36 Halloween and Fall Inspired Designs to color for fun
and relief from Stress, Anxiety & Depression

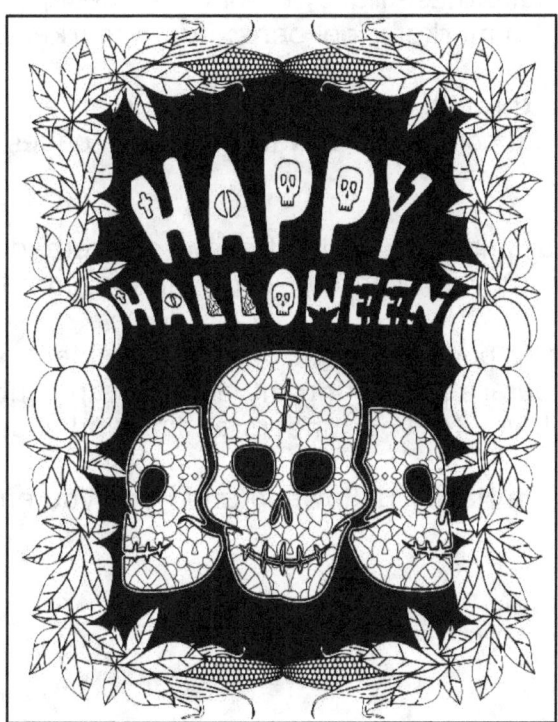

Cover and Book Design by Nerine Martin

www.ColorYourWayToHappy.com

ISBN-13: 978-1983562778
ISBN-10: 1983562777

A message from Nerine.....

Congratulations on your purchase of *'Happy Halloween'* a fun coloring book for the whole family to enjoy, and thank you for choosing my coloring book.

Inside this fun and spooky coloring book, you will find 36 unique Halloween and Fall inspired designs that the whole family can come together on Halloween to color.

Use your imagination to make these Halloween holiday designs come alive with color, using colored pencils, felt tip markers, gel pens, fluoro markers, metallic pens or crayons.

To help prevent any bleed through when using felt tip markers – place a blank sheet of paper behind the page when coloring. You will find spare pages at the back of this book you can tear out and use.

Please remember that your purchase of this Halloween themed coloring book is for your personal use only and you may not share or copy the uncolored pages for others.

Please direct other people to purchase their own, or consider giving them a copy as a lovely gift. By doing so, you are supporting my art so I can continue to make more coloring books and I thank you for your understanding and support. ☺

I wish you and your family a Happy Halloween and hope you enjoy coloring this book.

Trick or Treat!

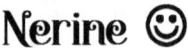 ☺

Use This Area To Test Your Colors

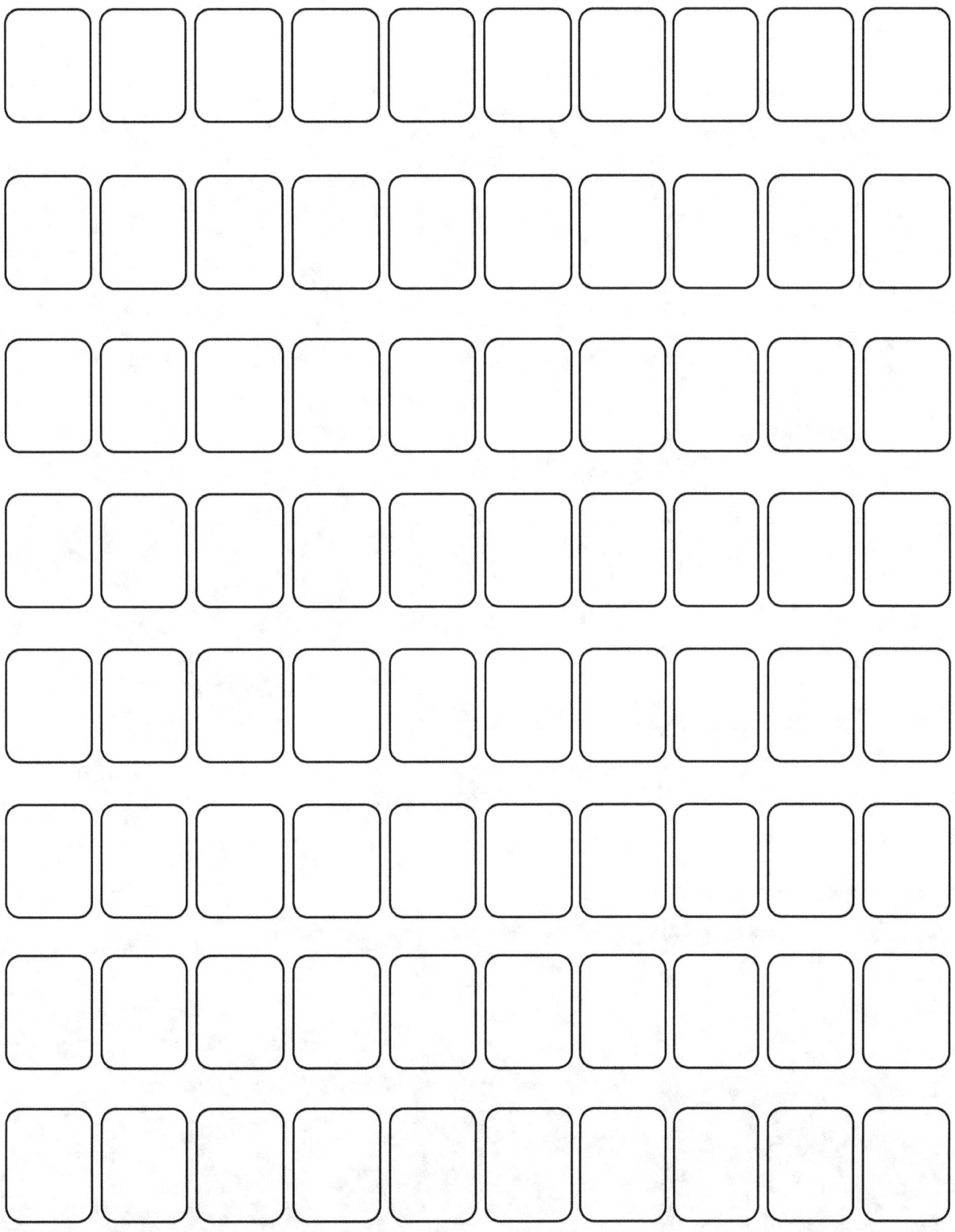

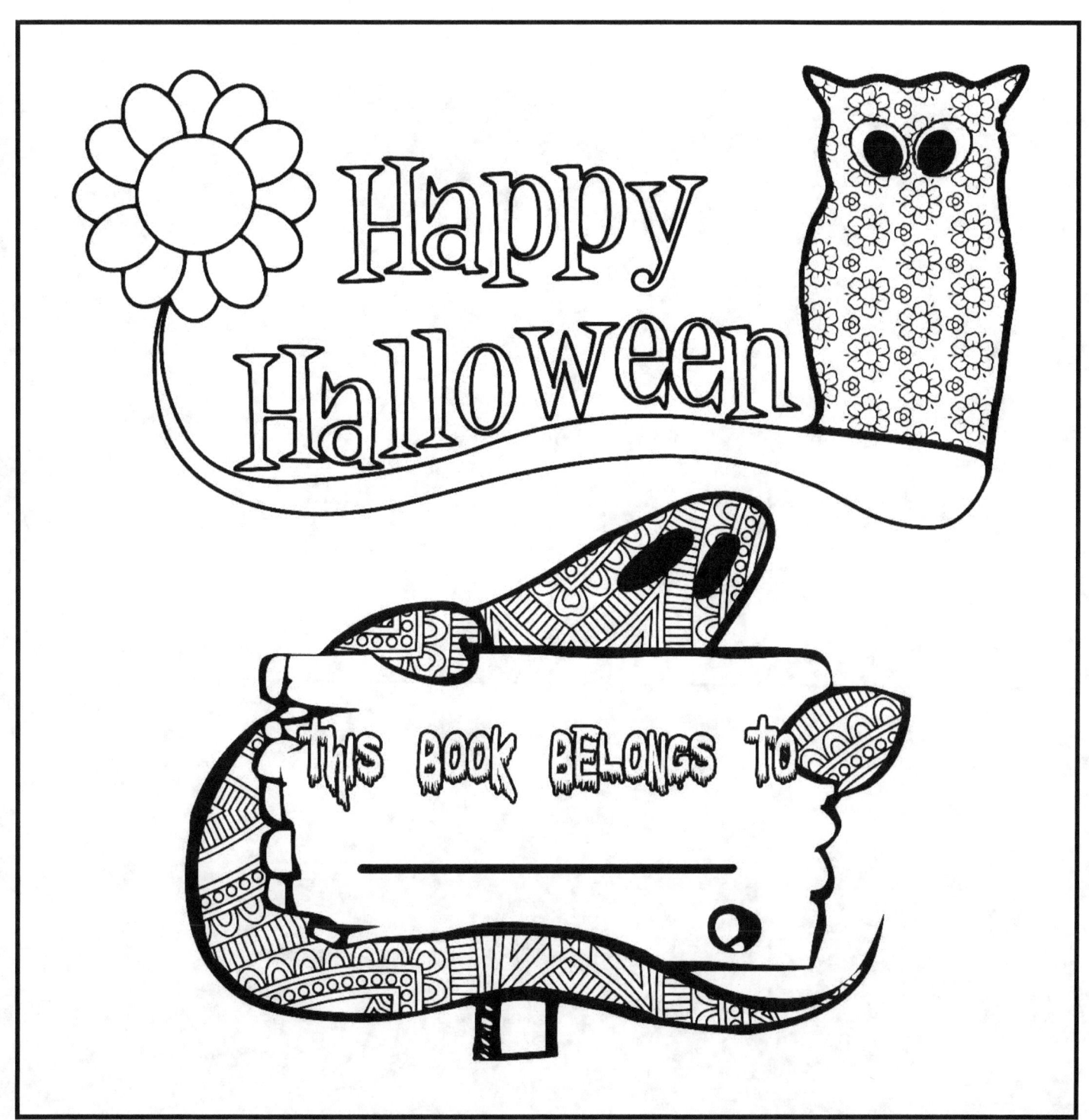

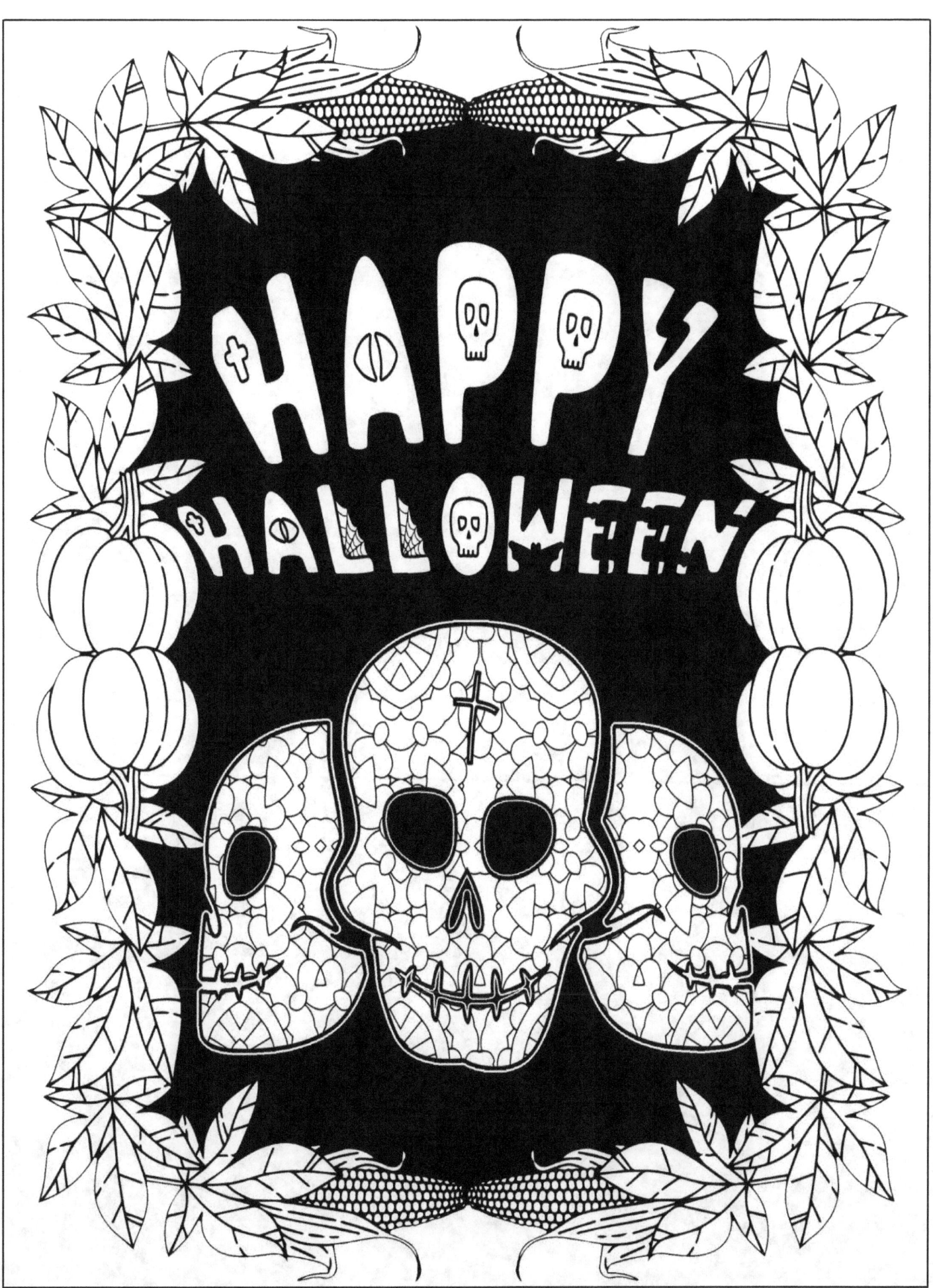

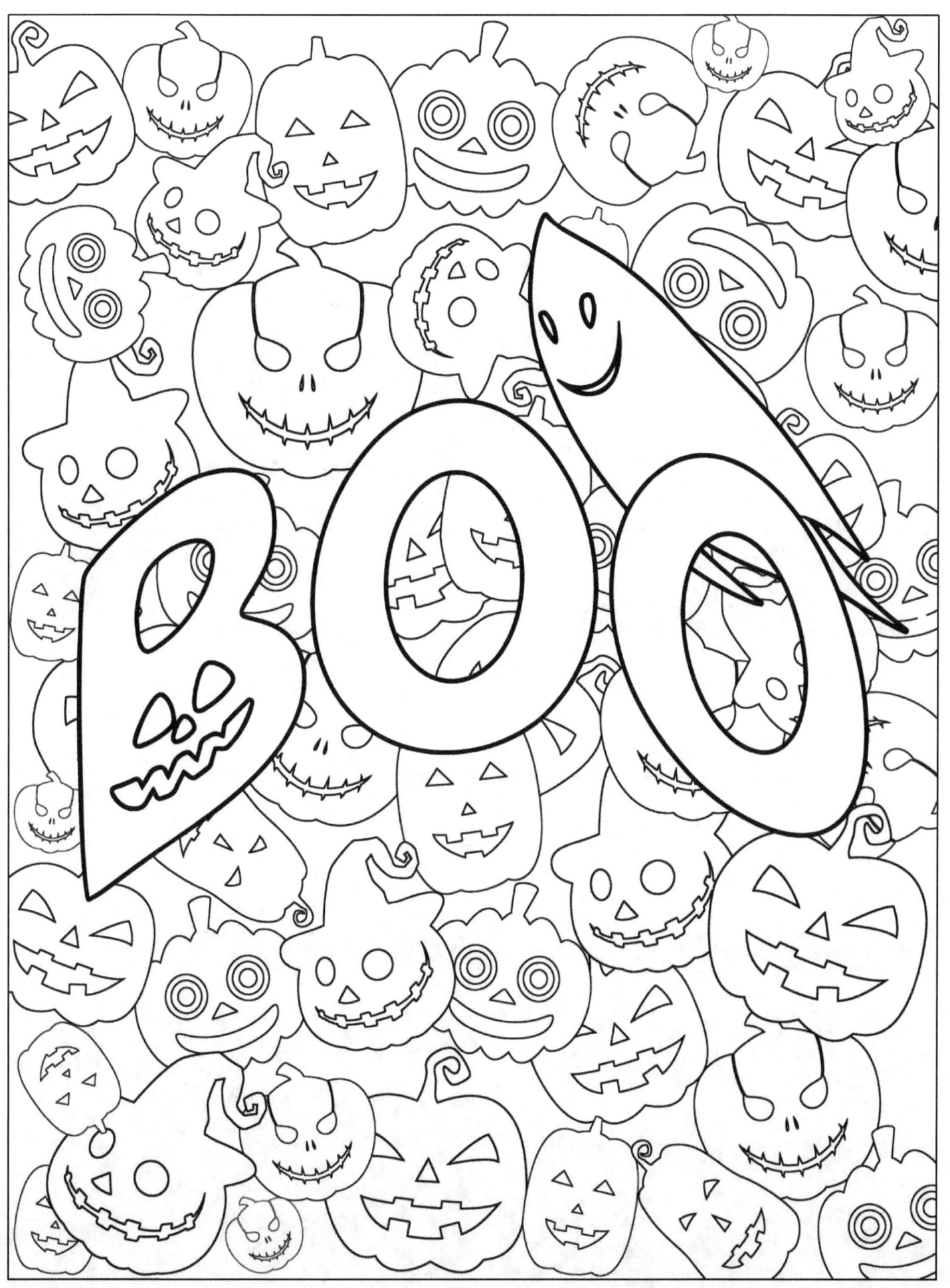

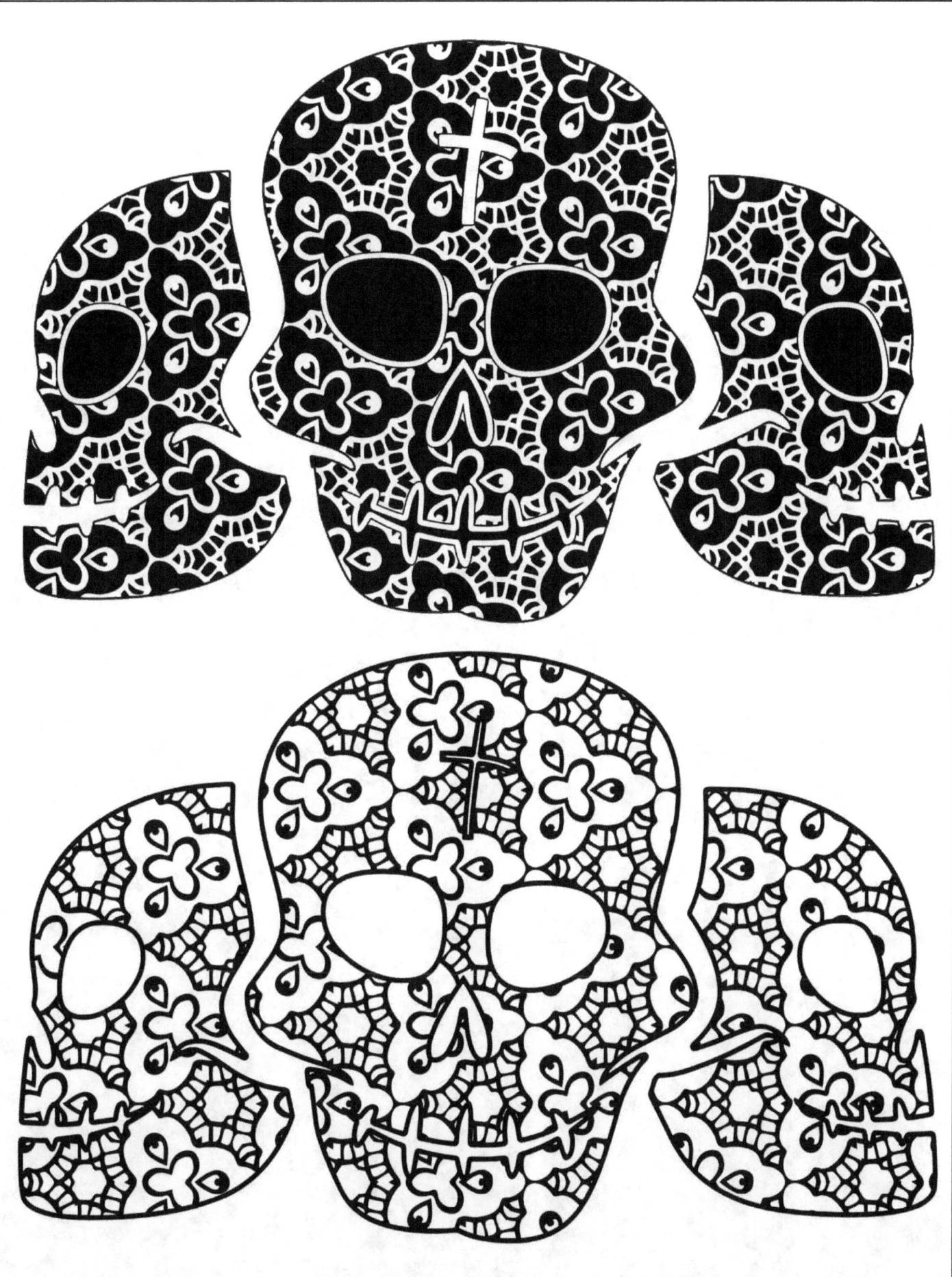

GHOSTS HAVE REAL SPIRIT

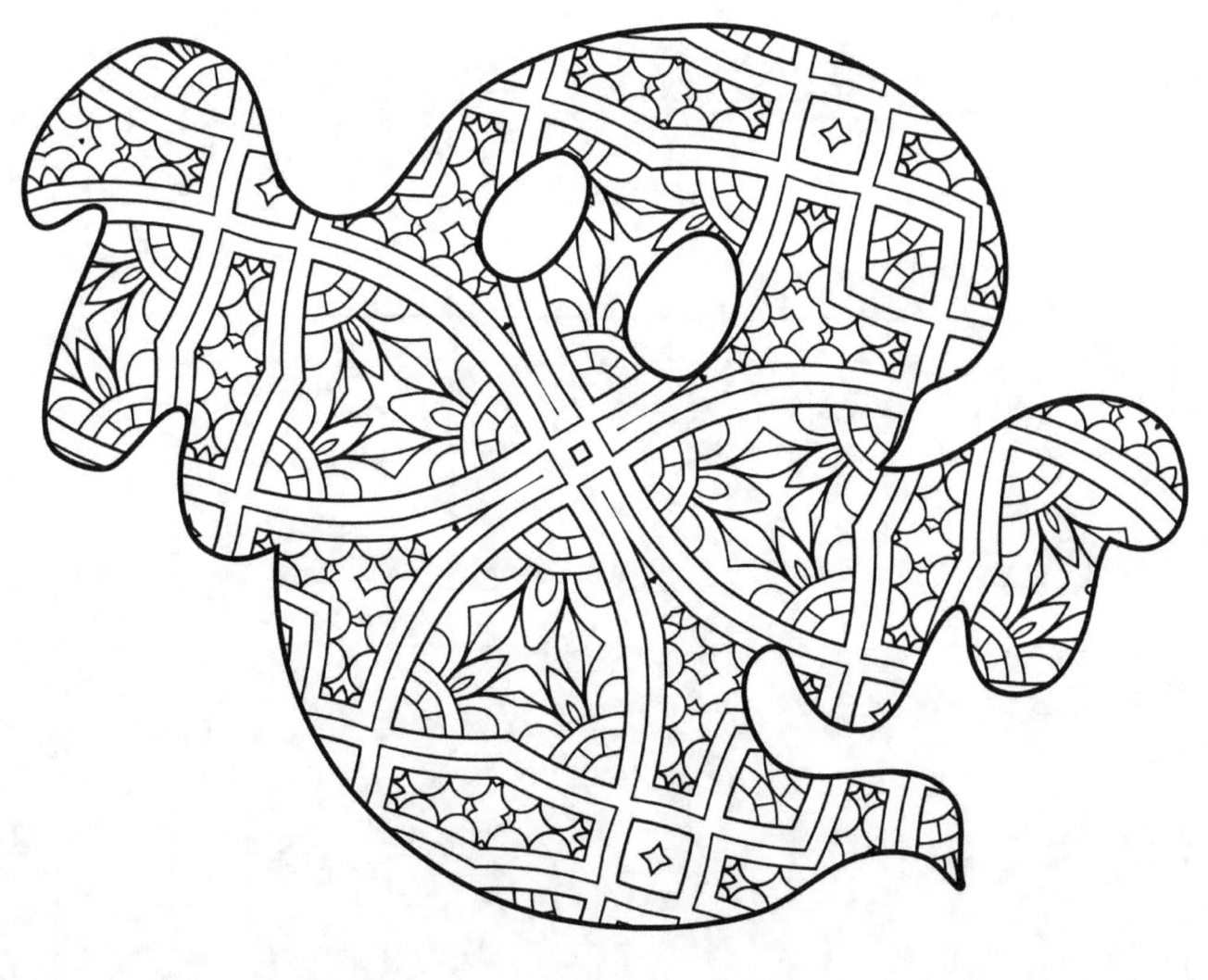

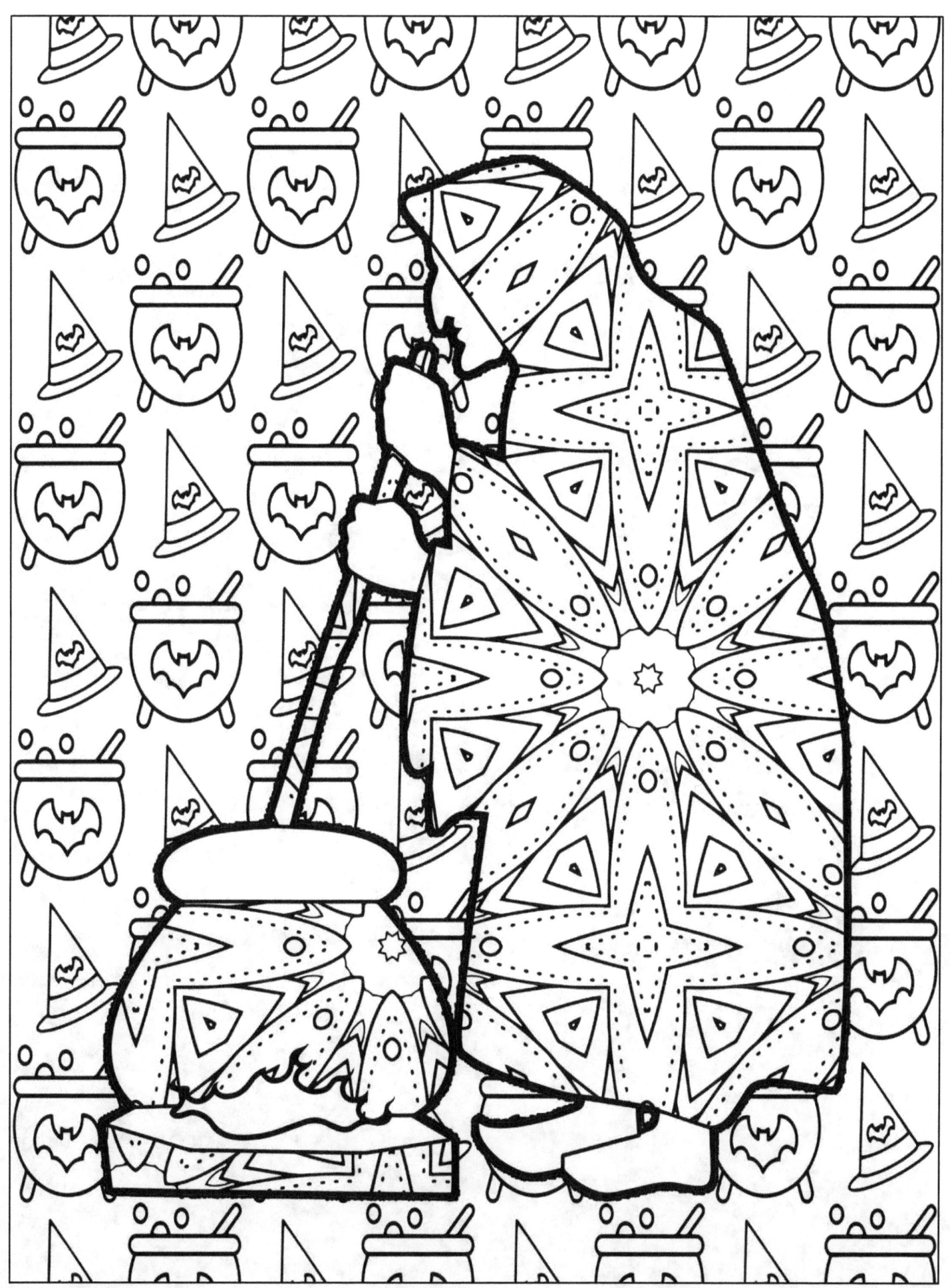

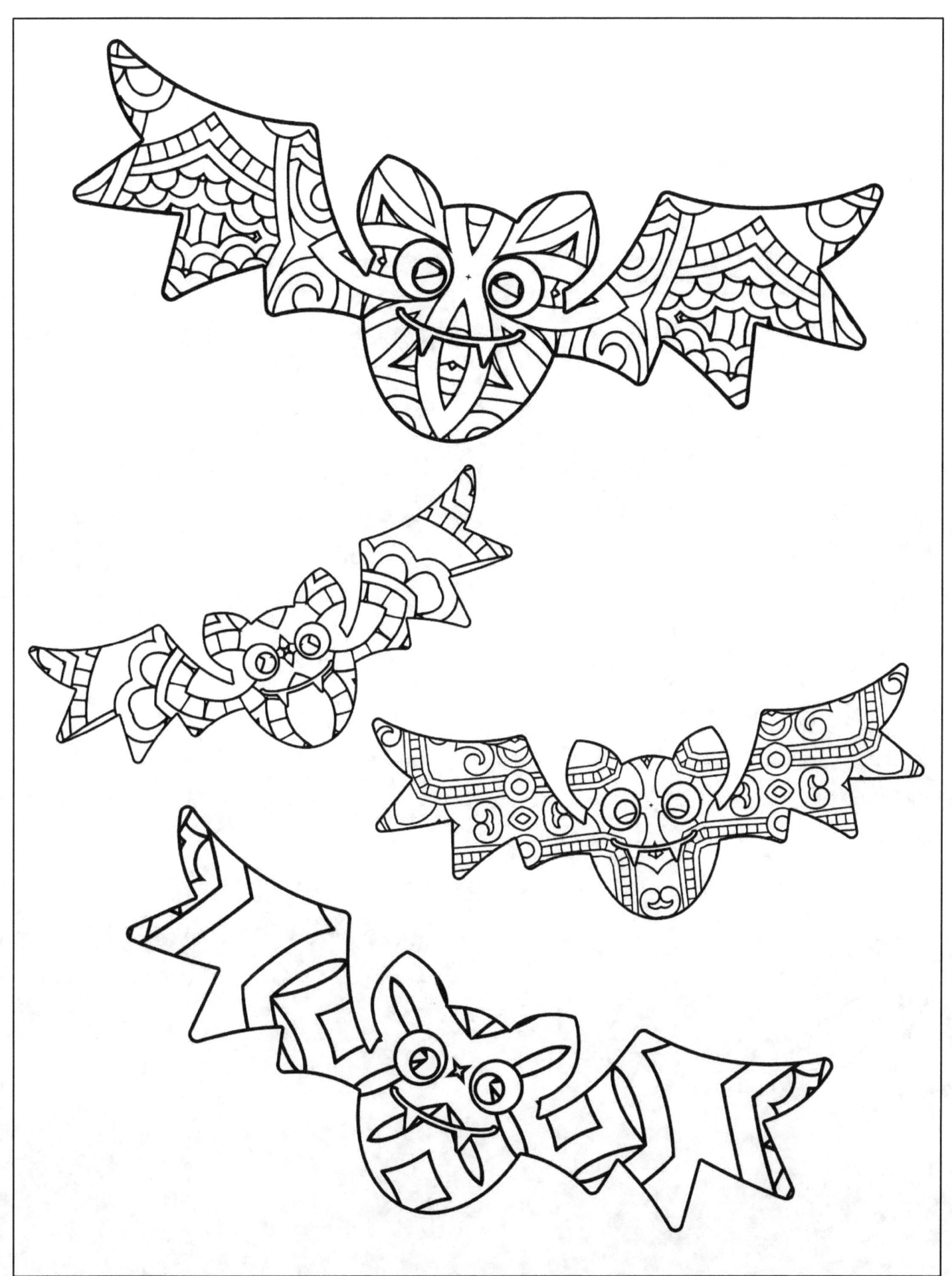

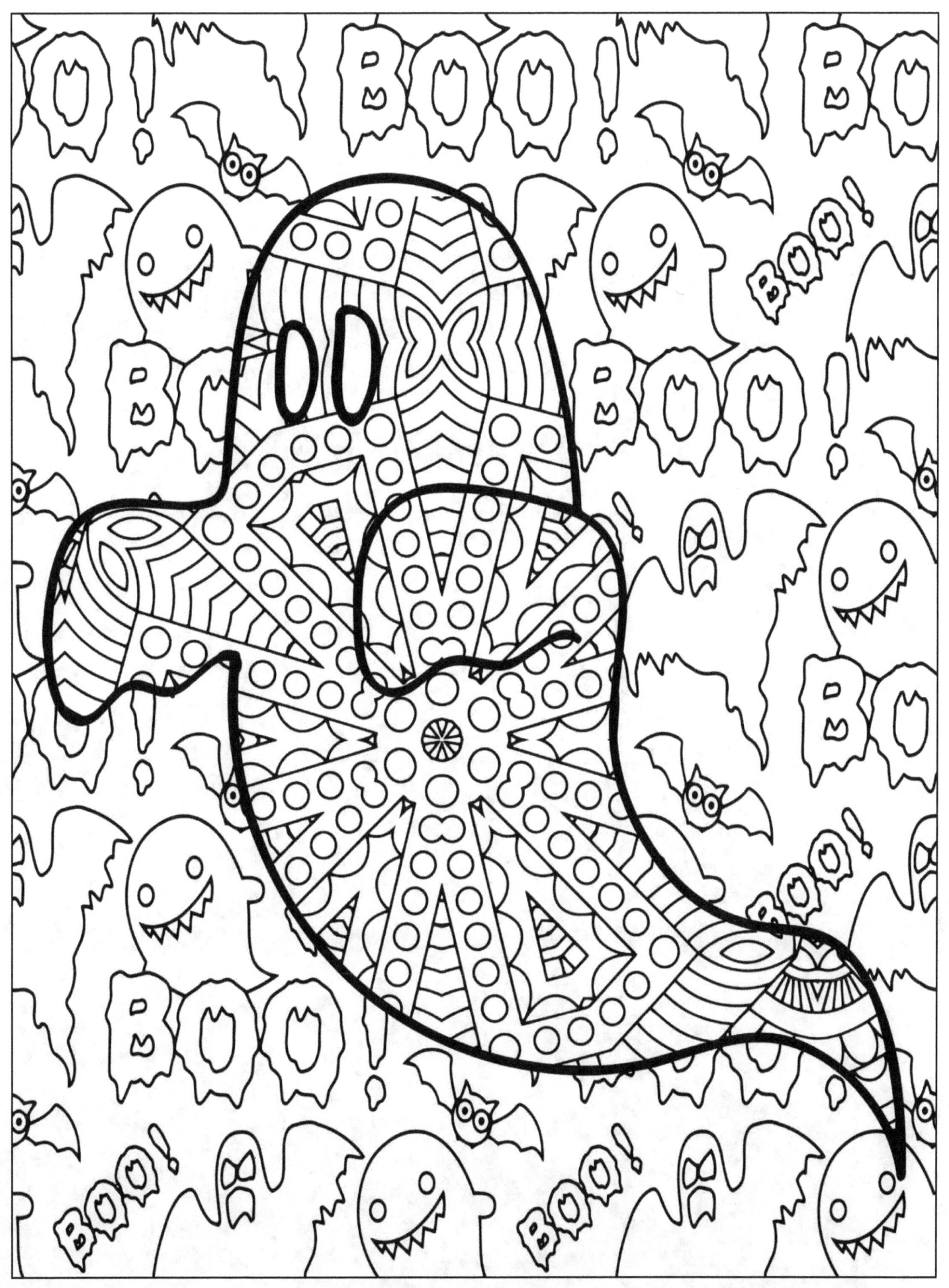

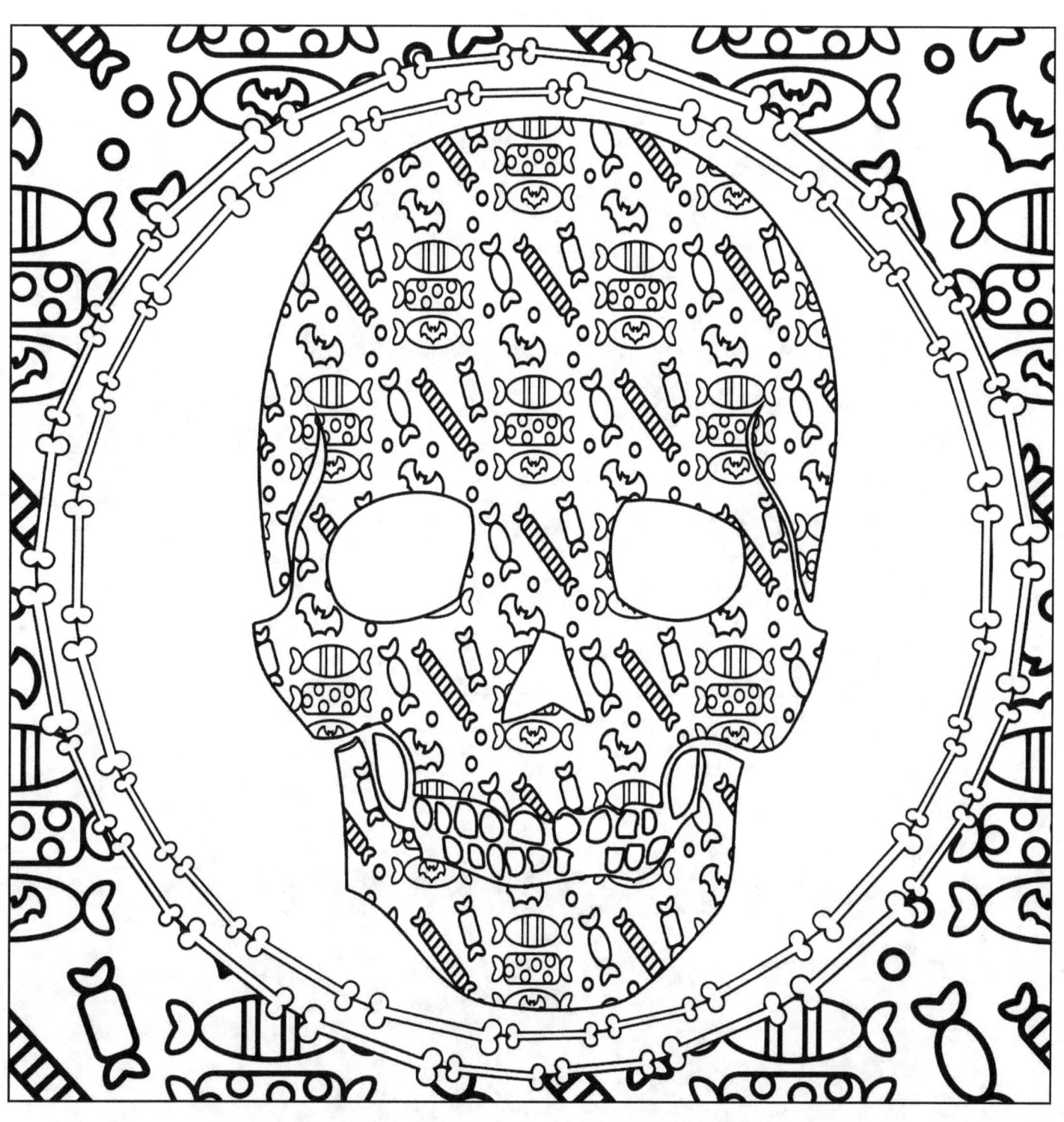

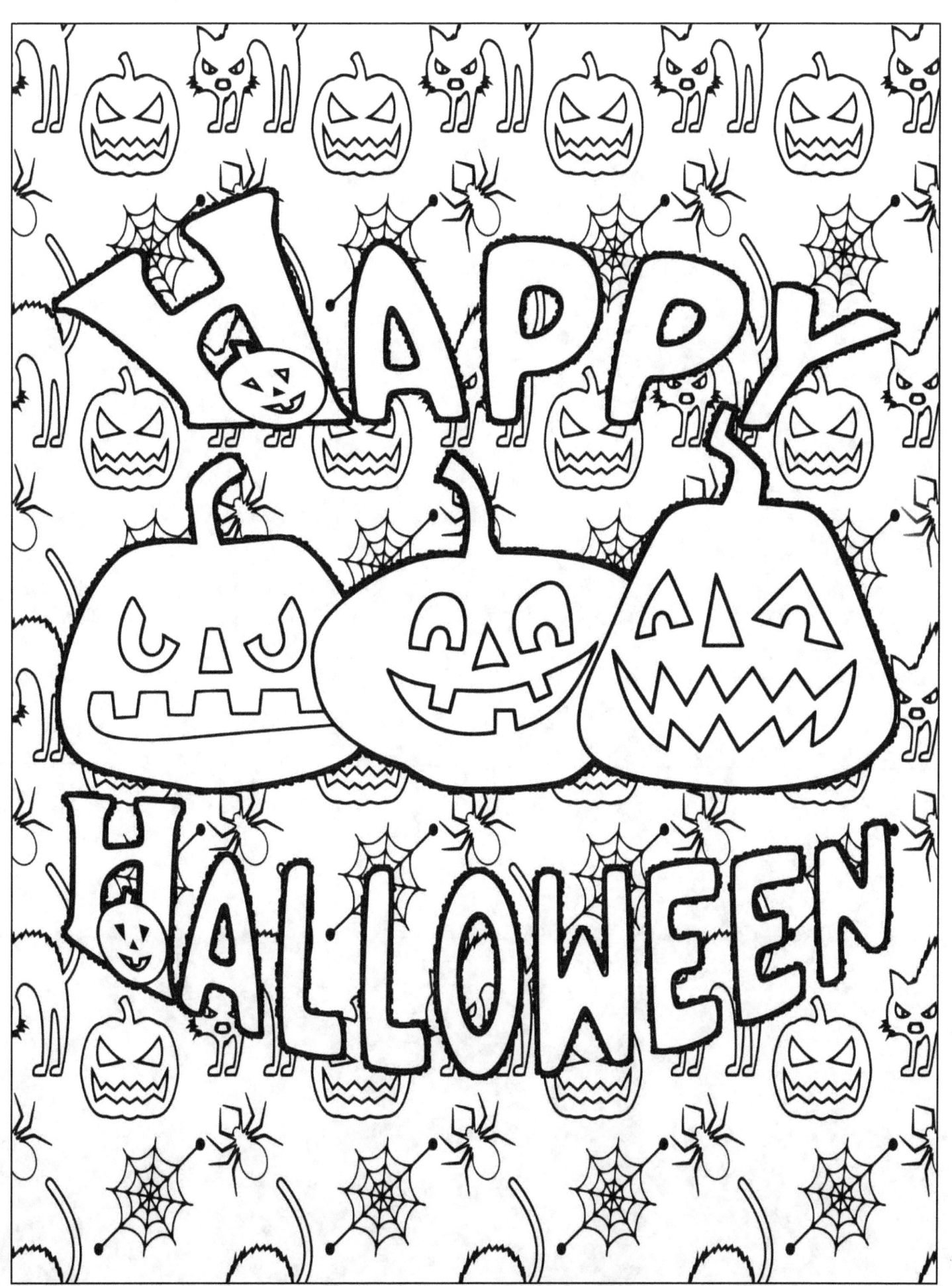

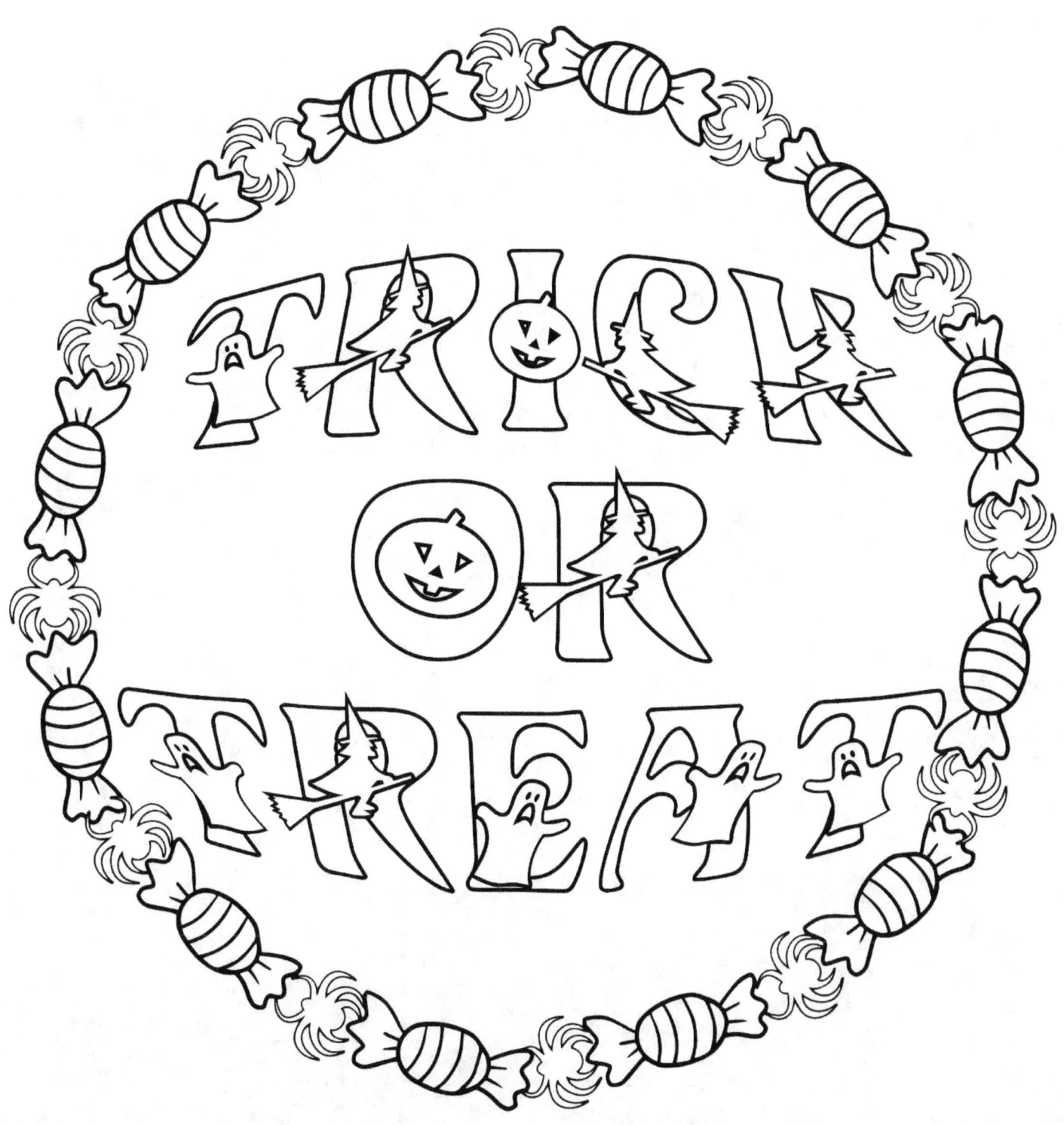

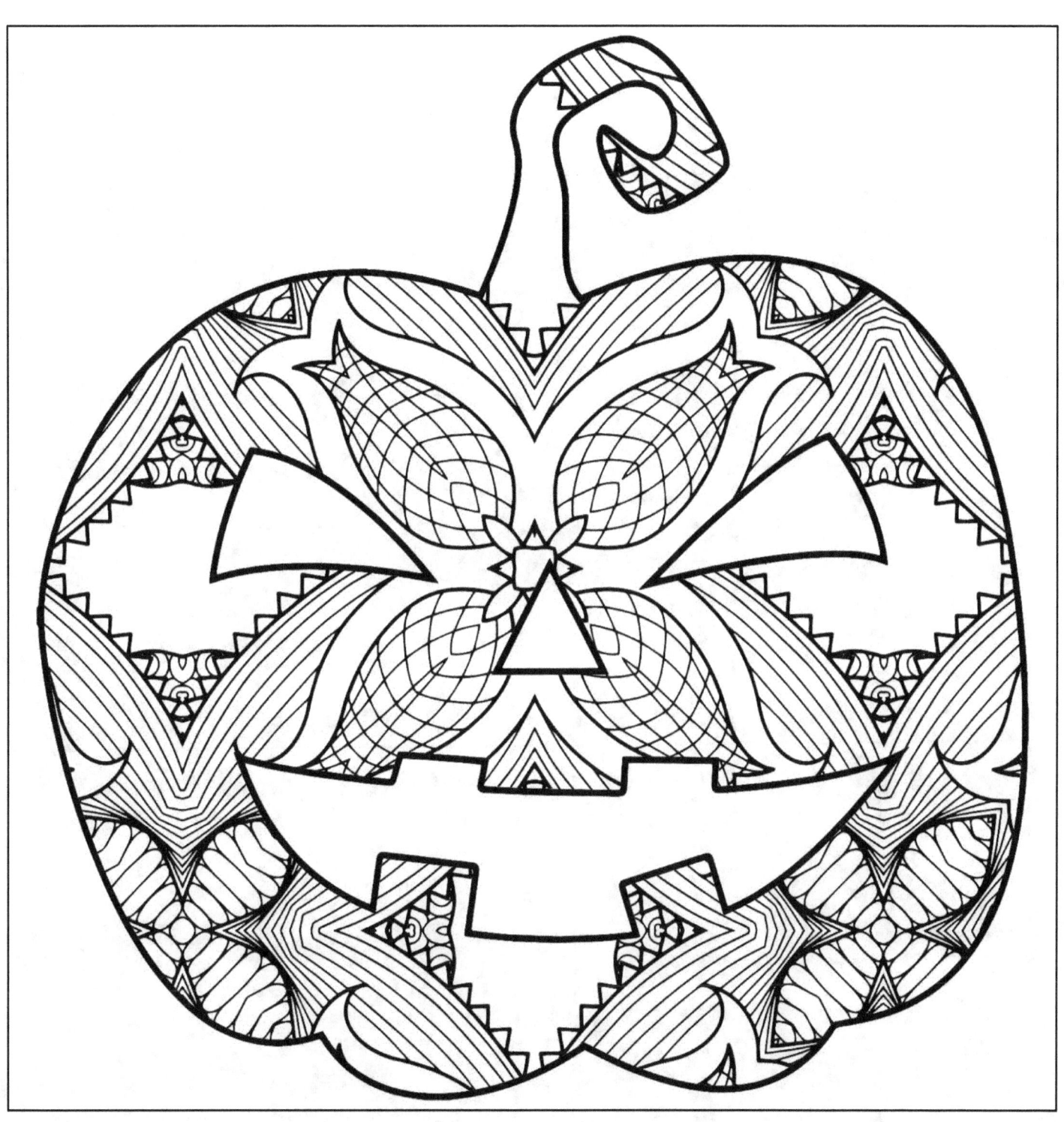

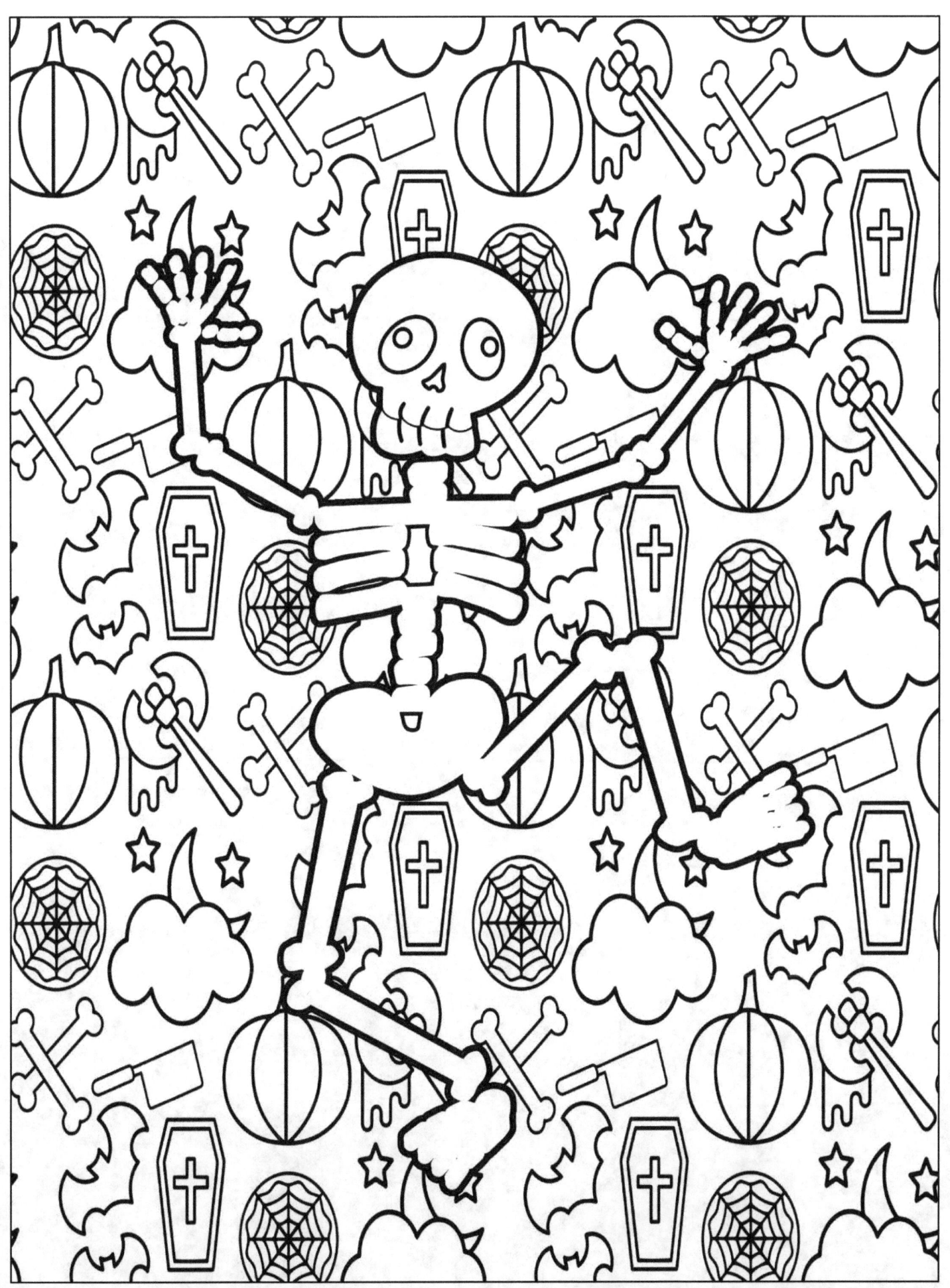

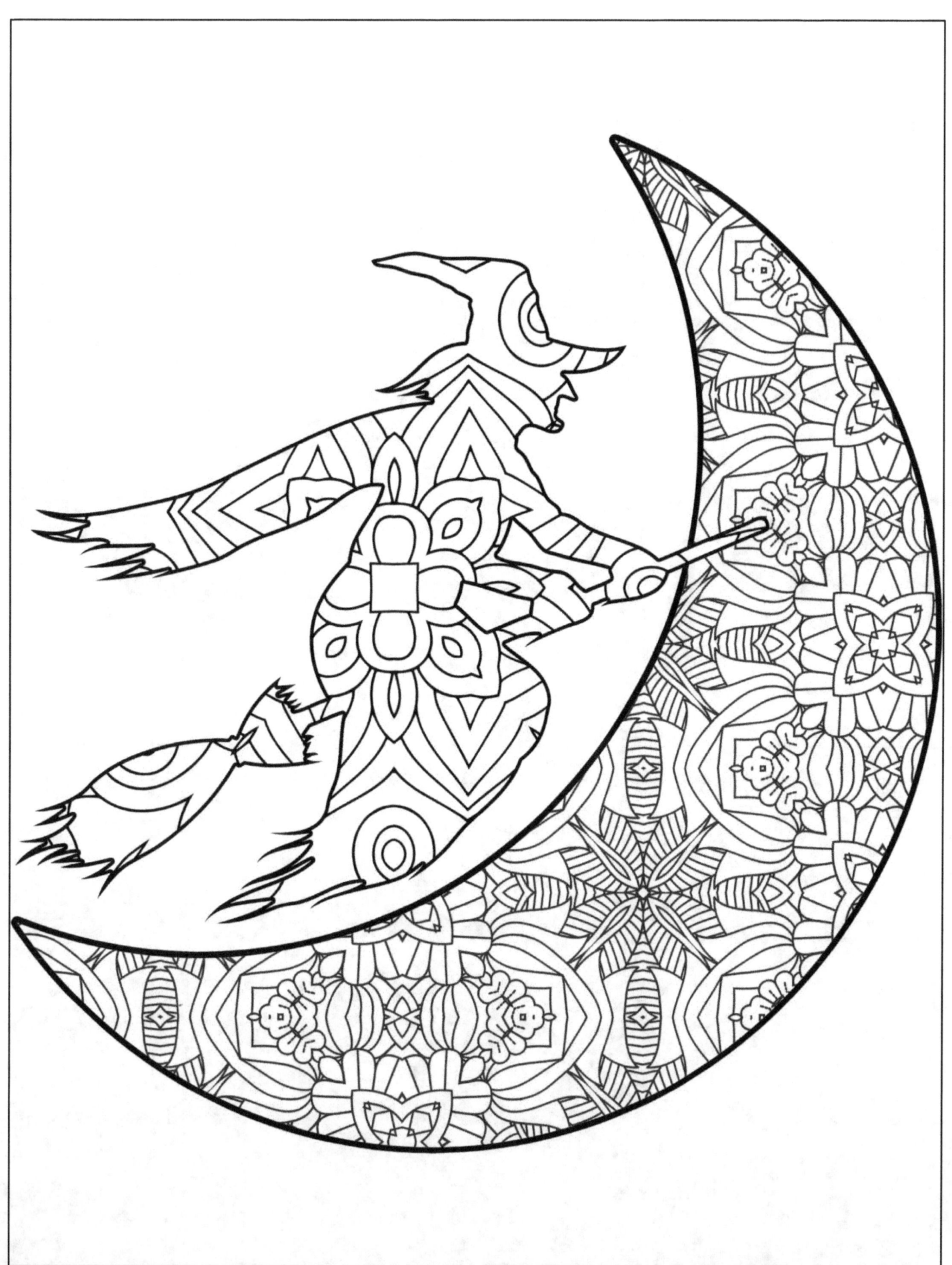

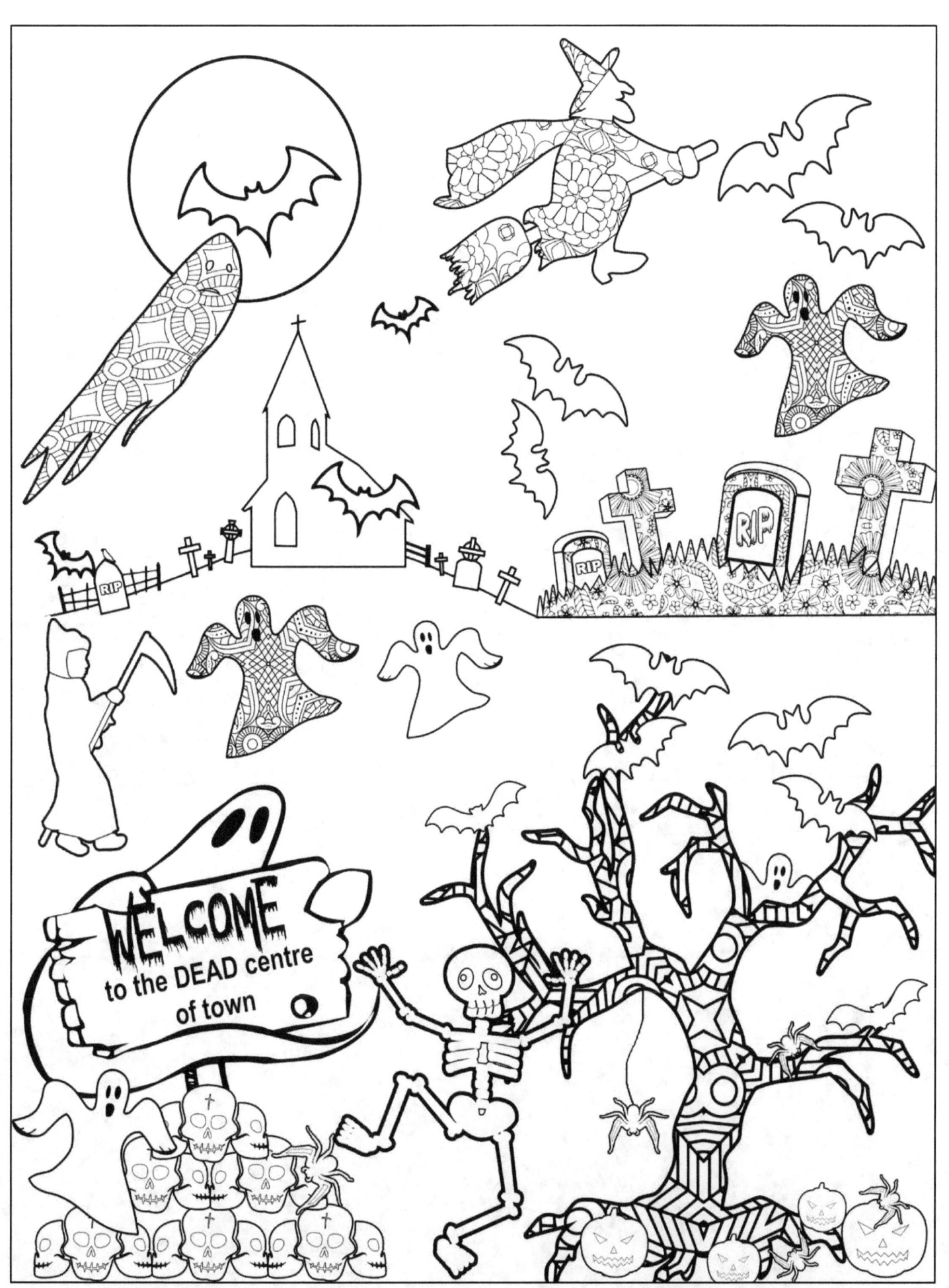

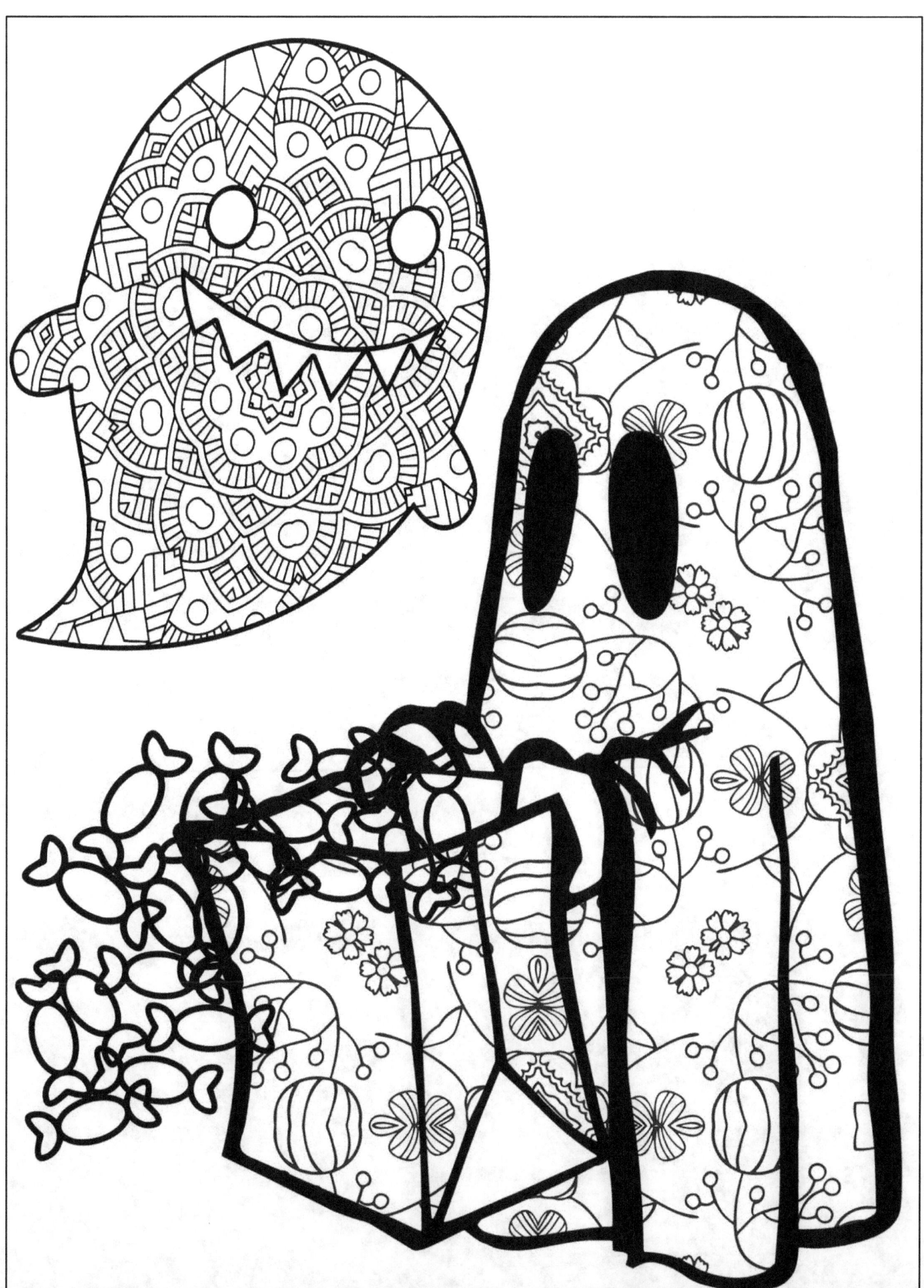

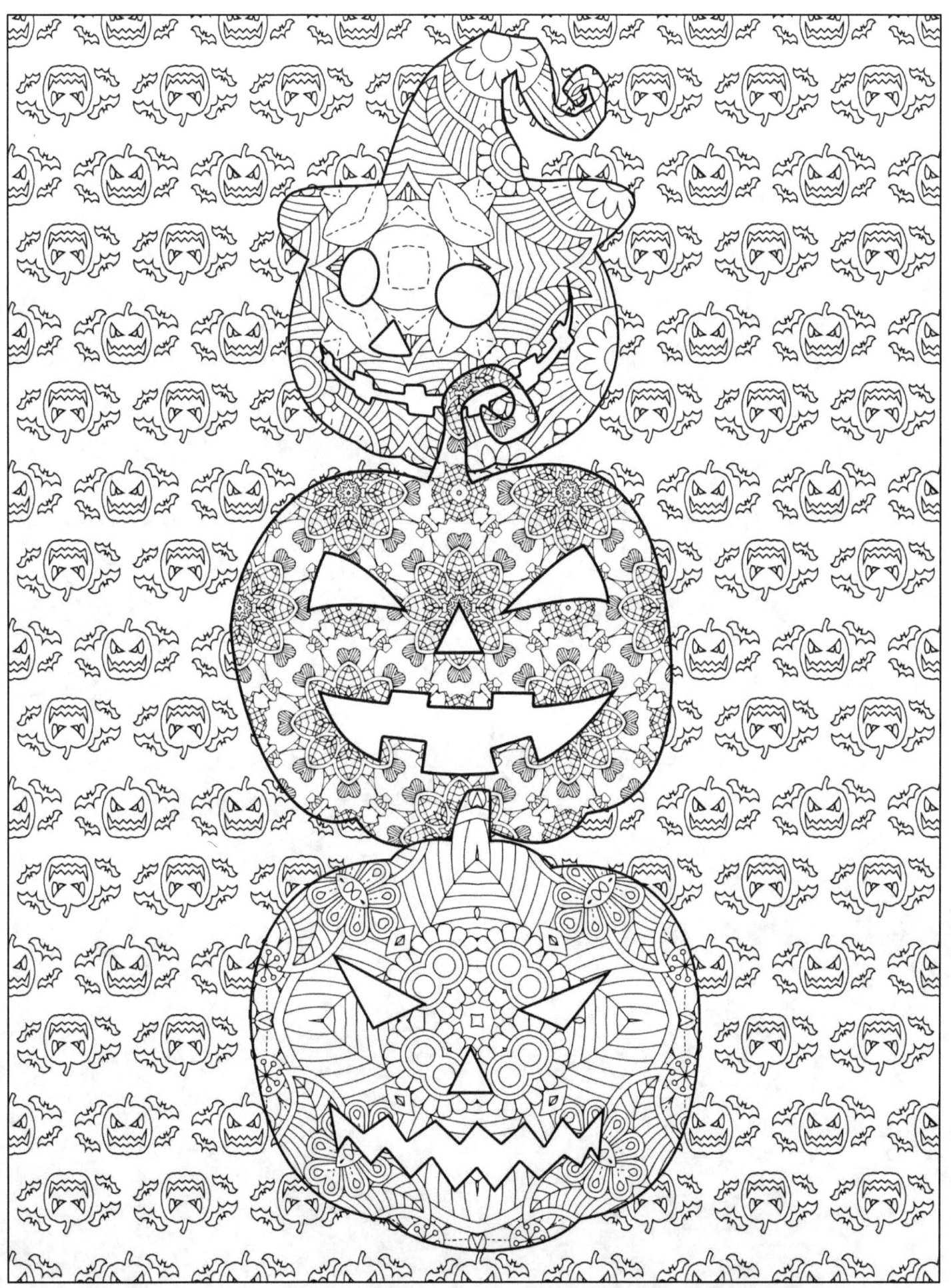

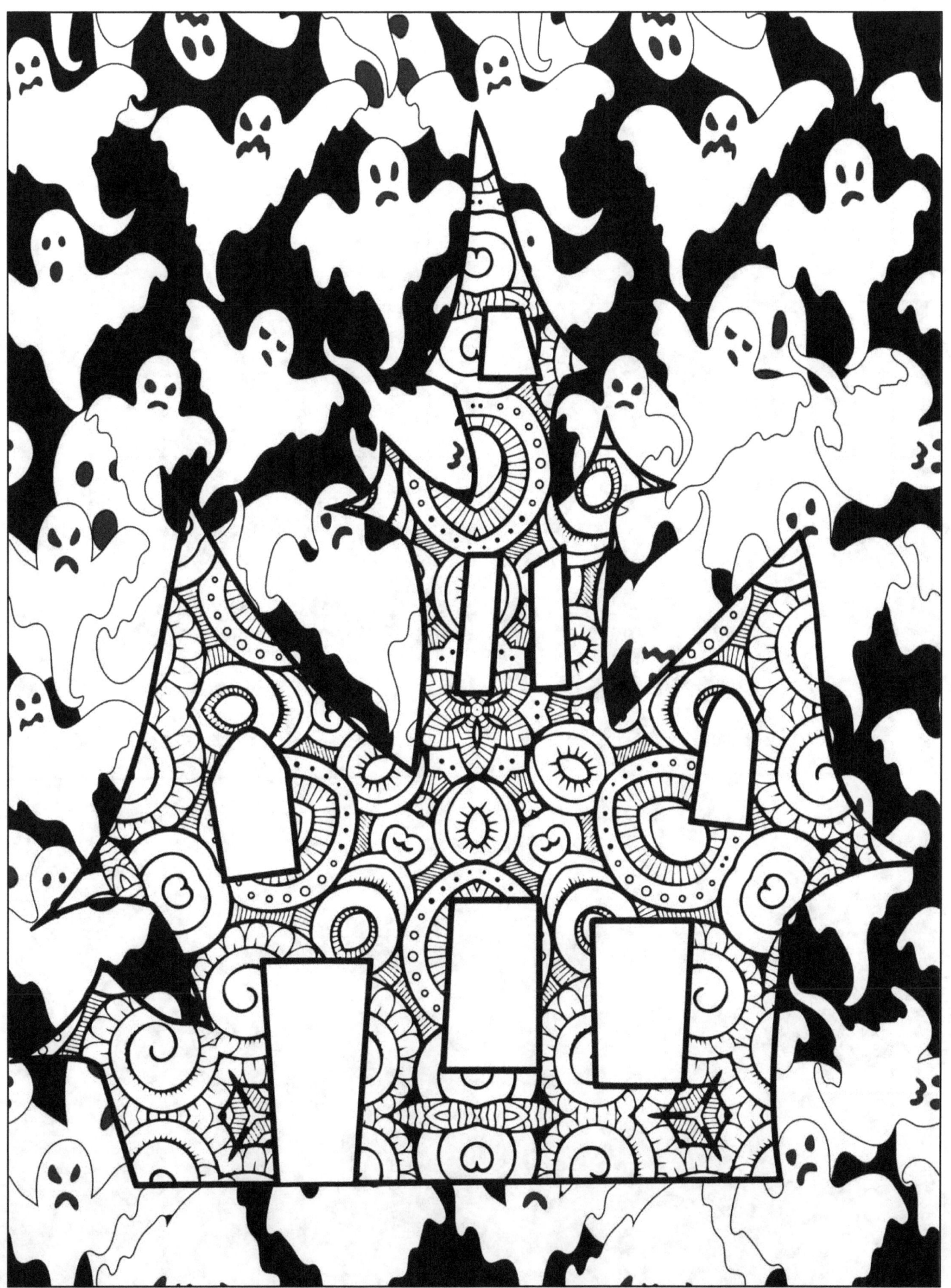

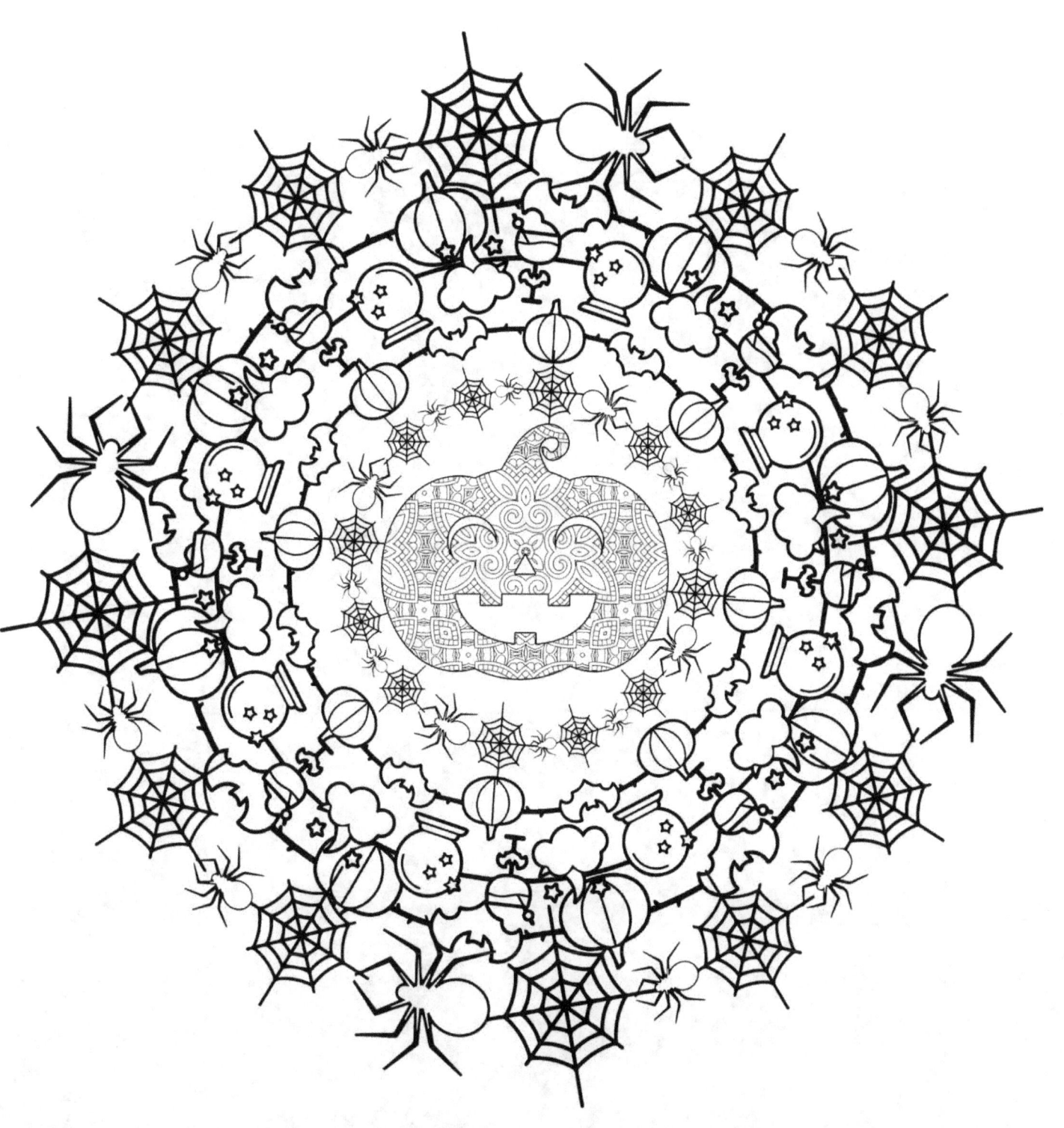

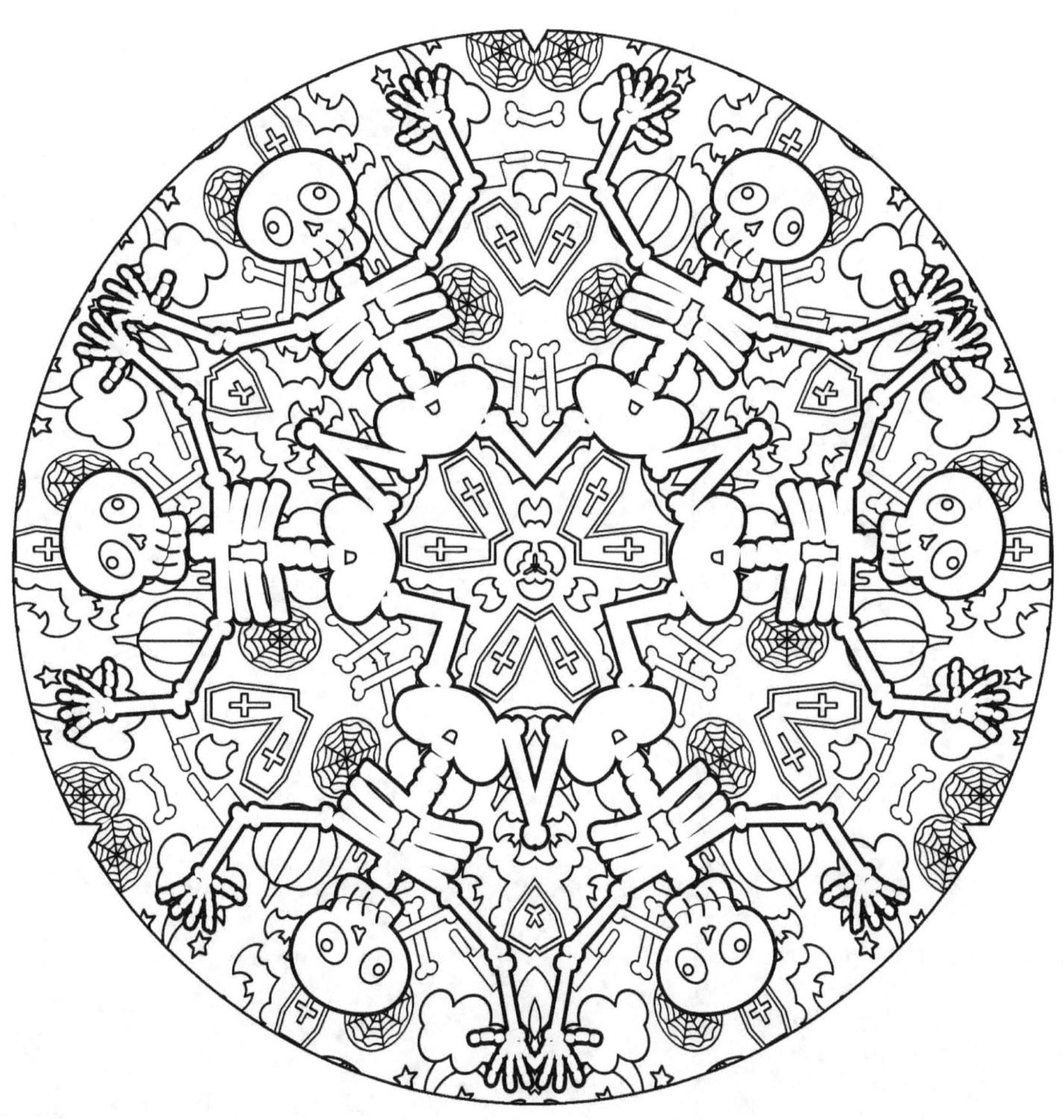

IF THE BROOM FITS

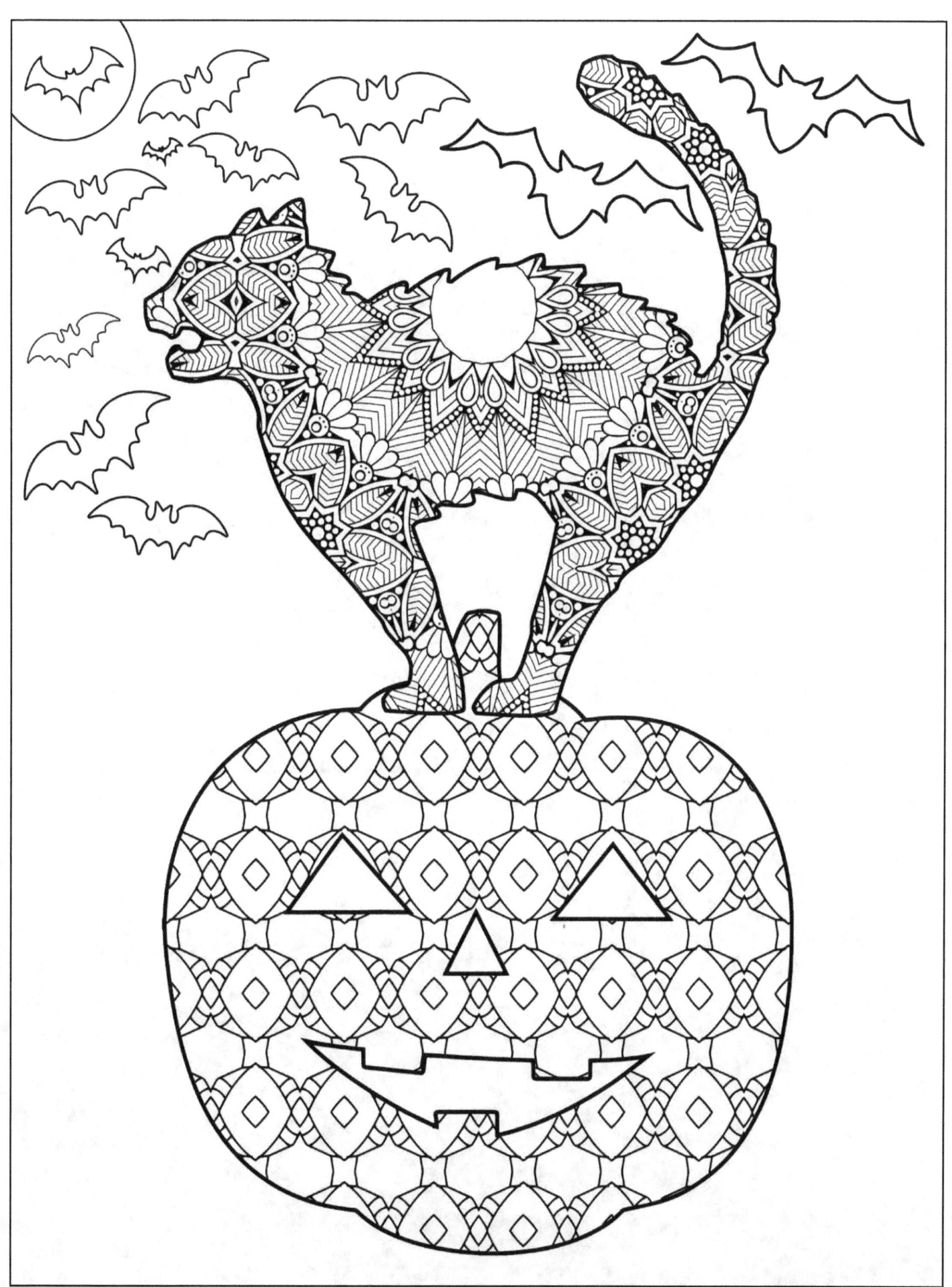

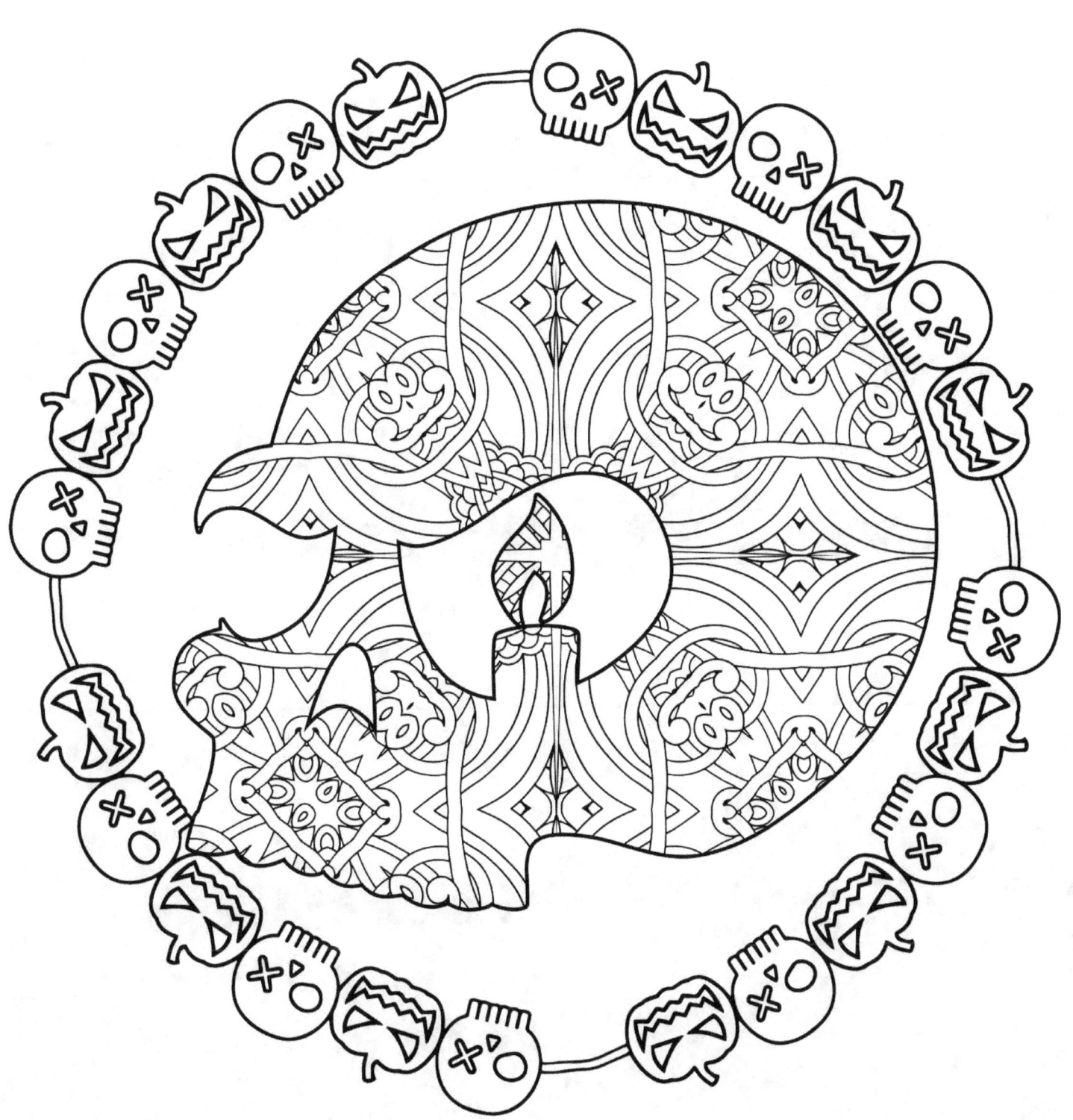

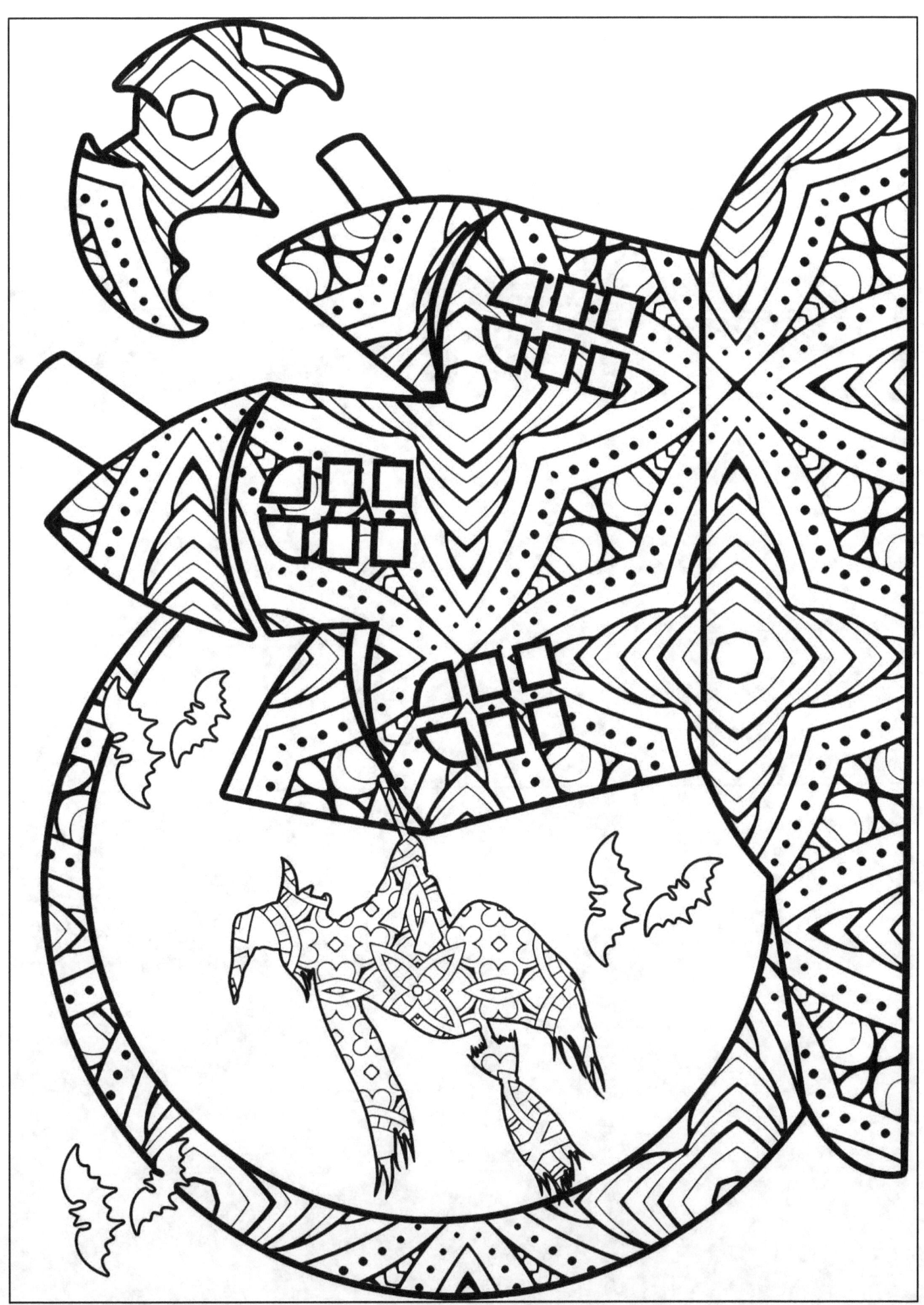

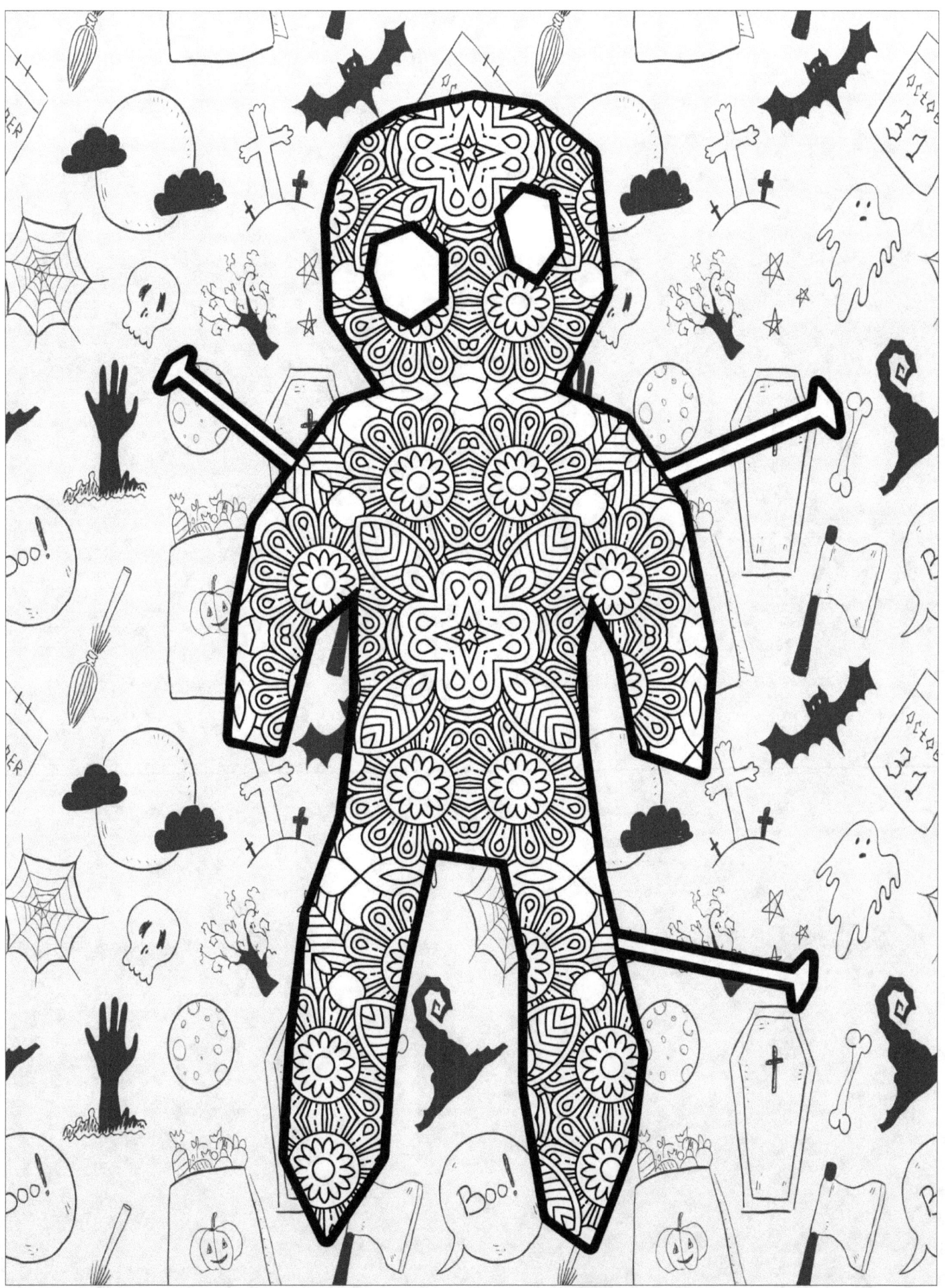

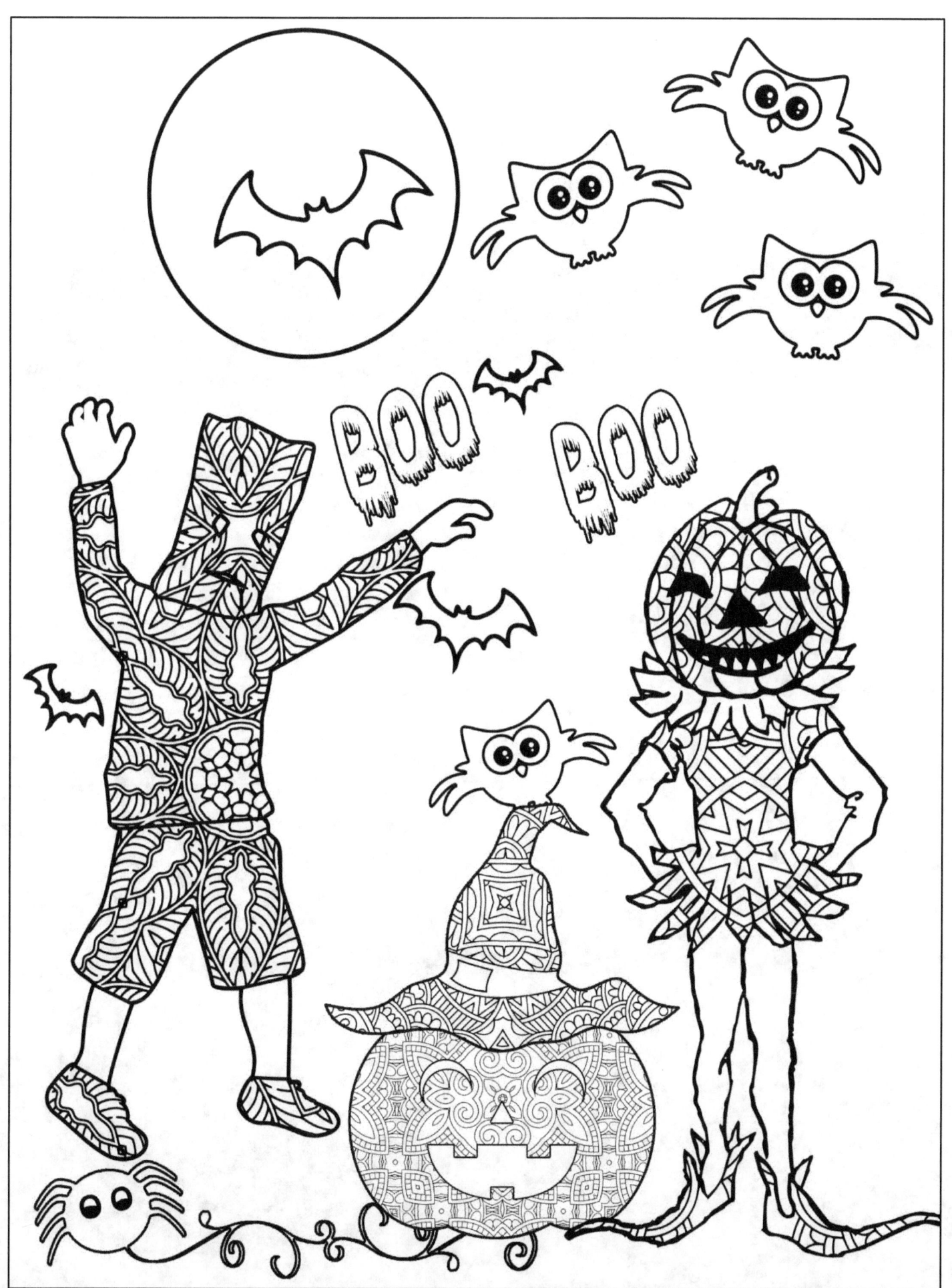

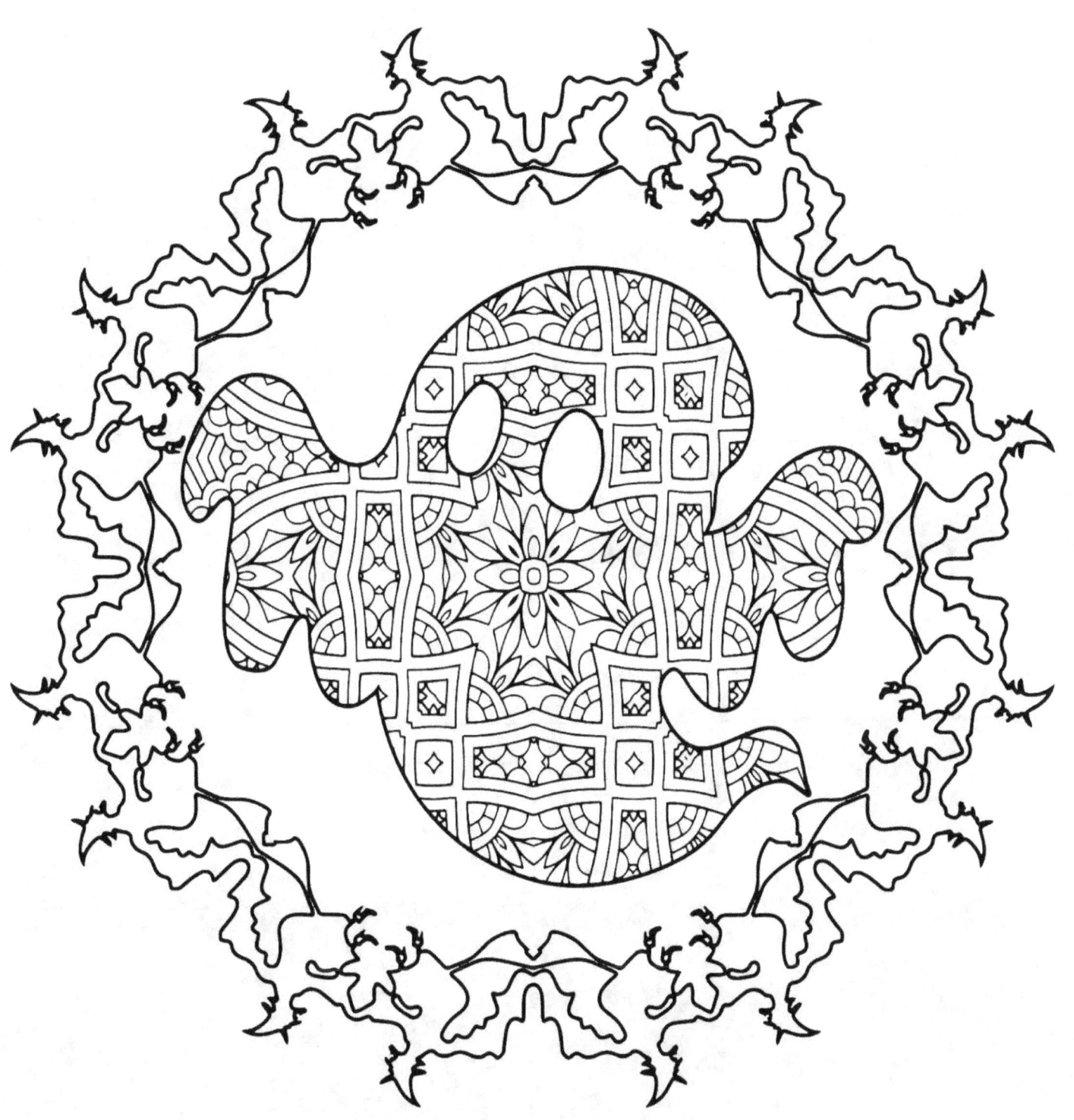

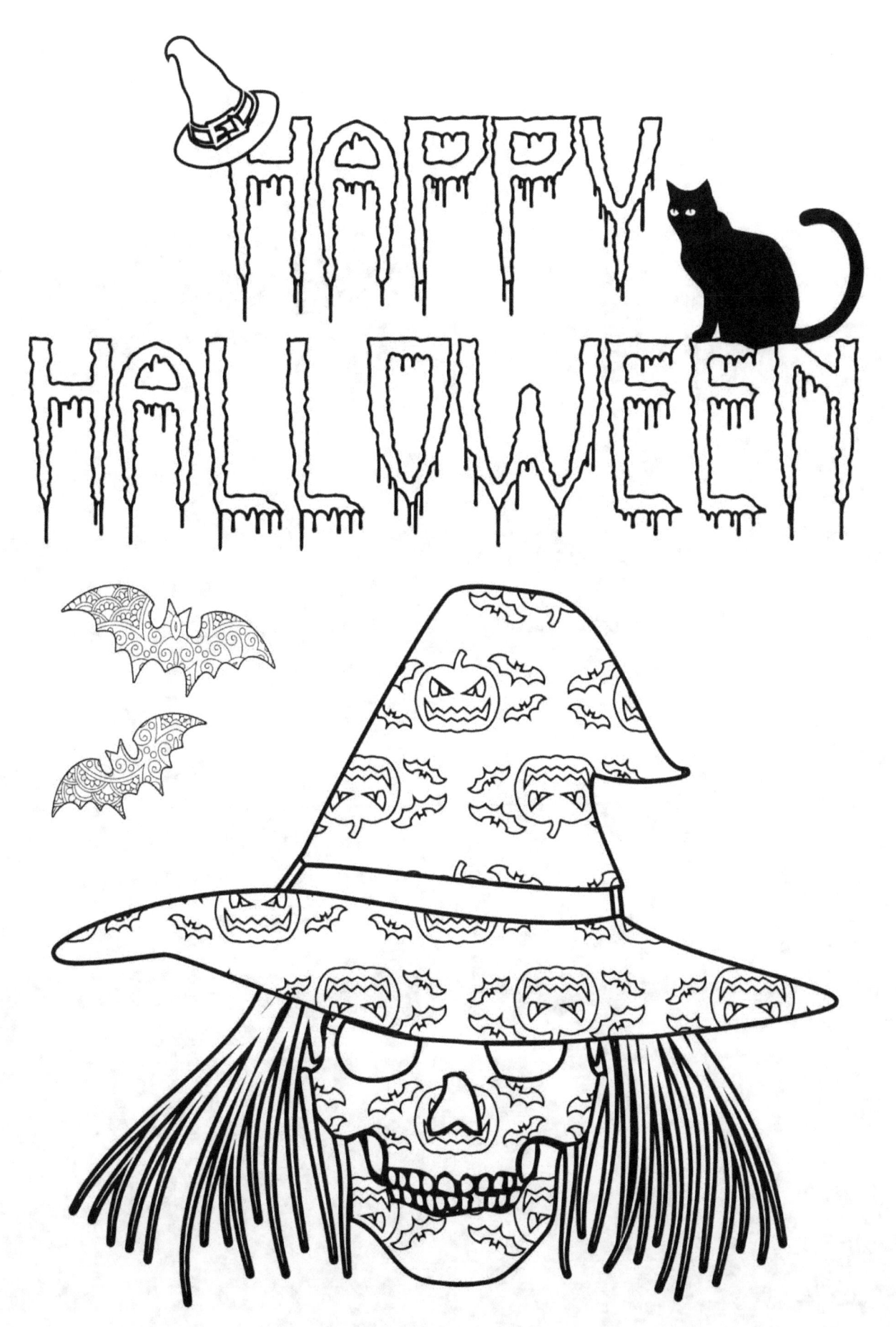

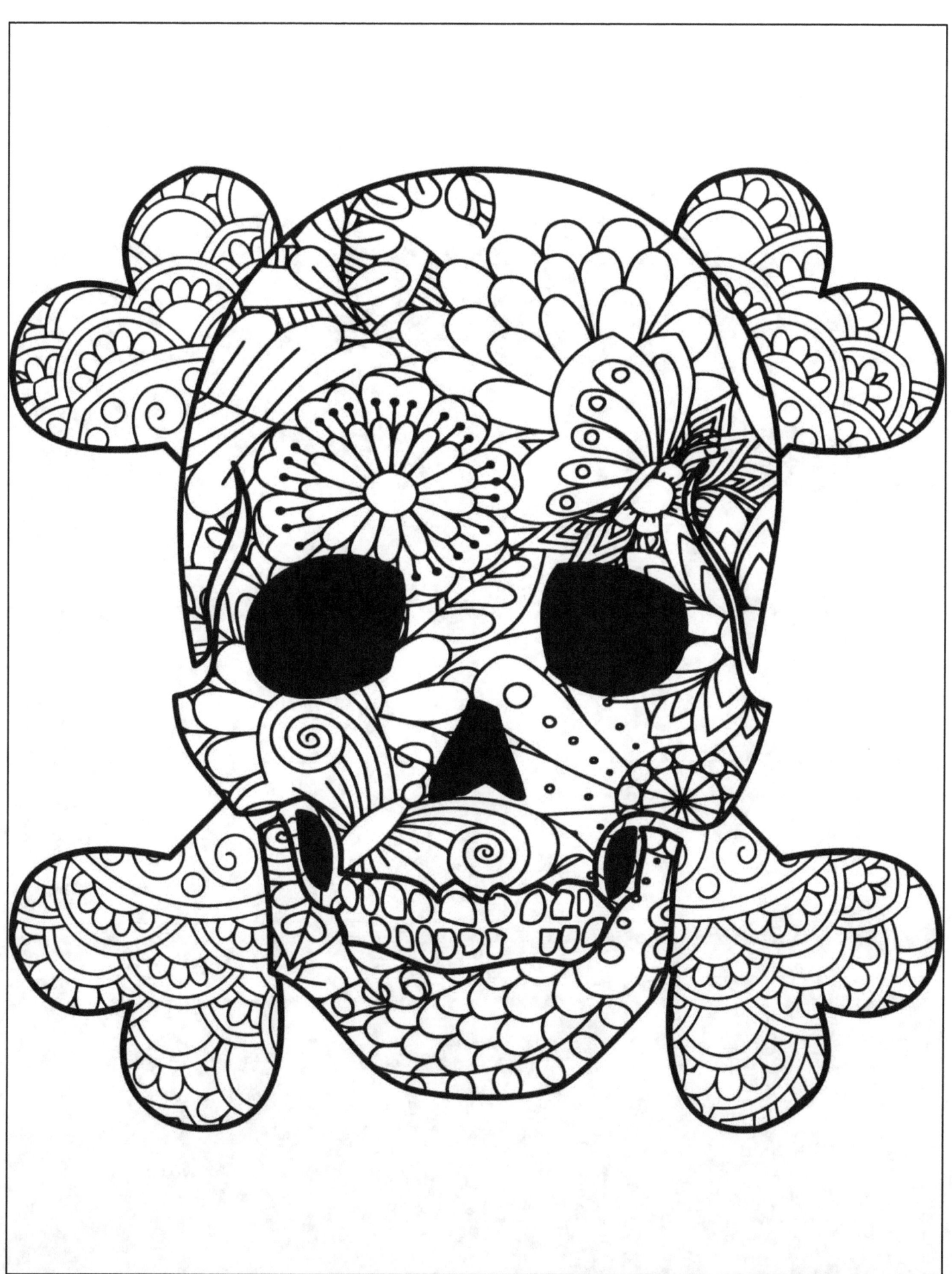

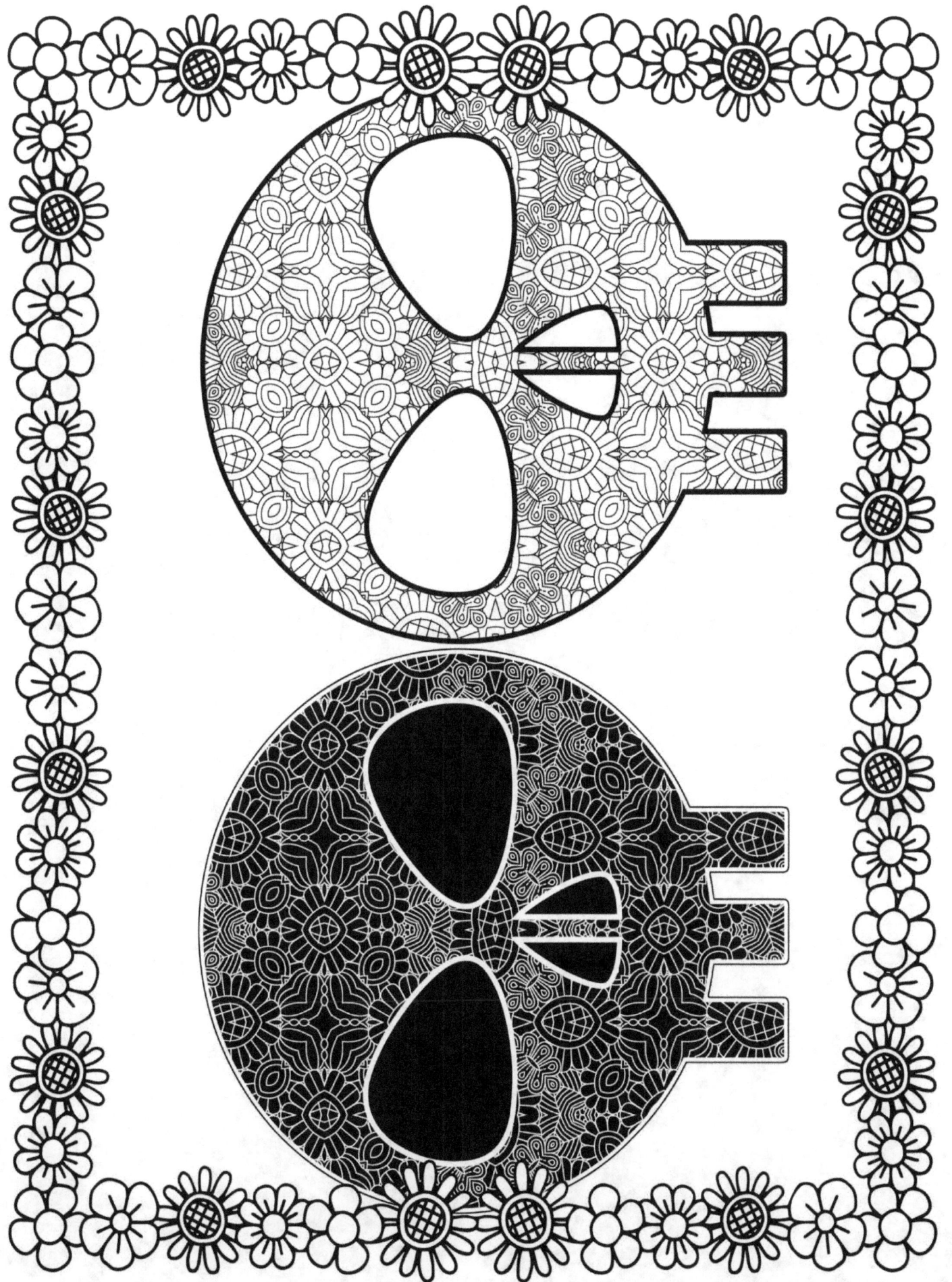

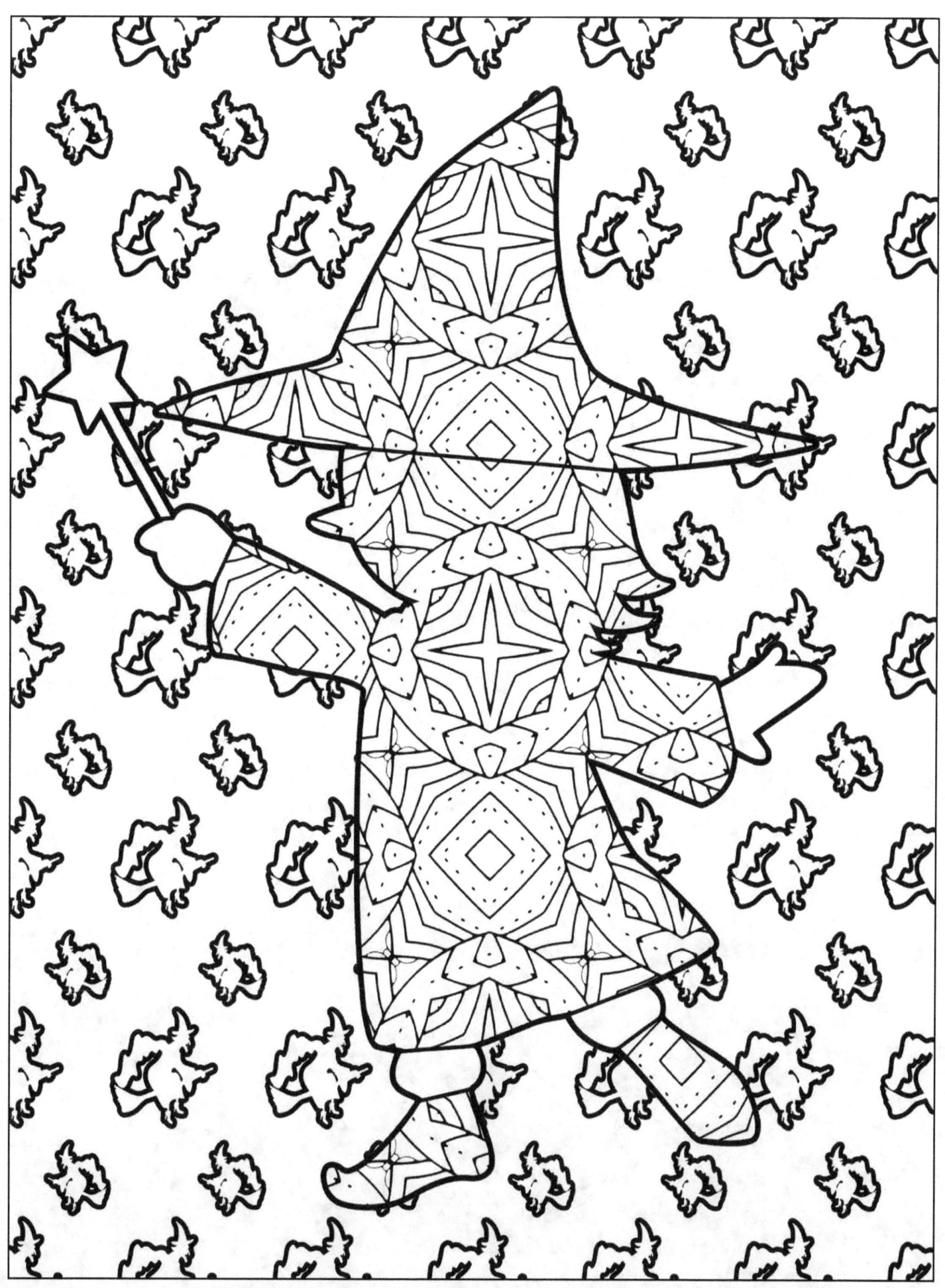

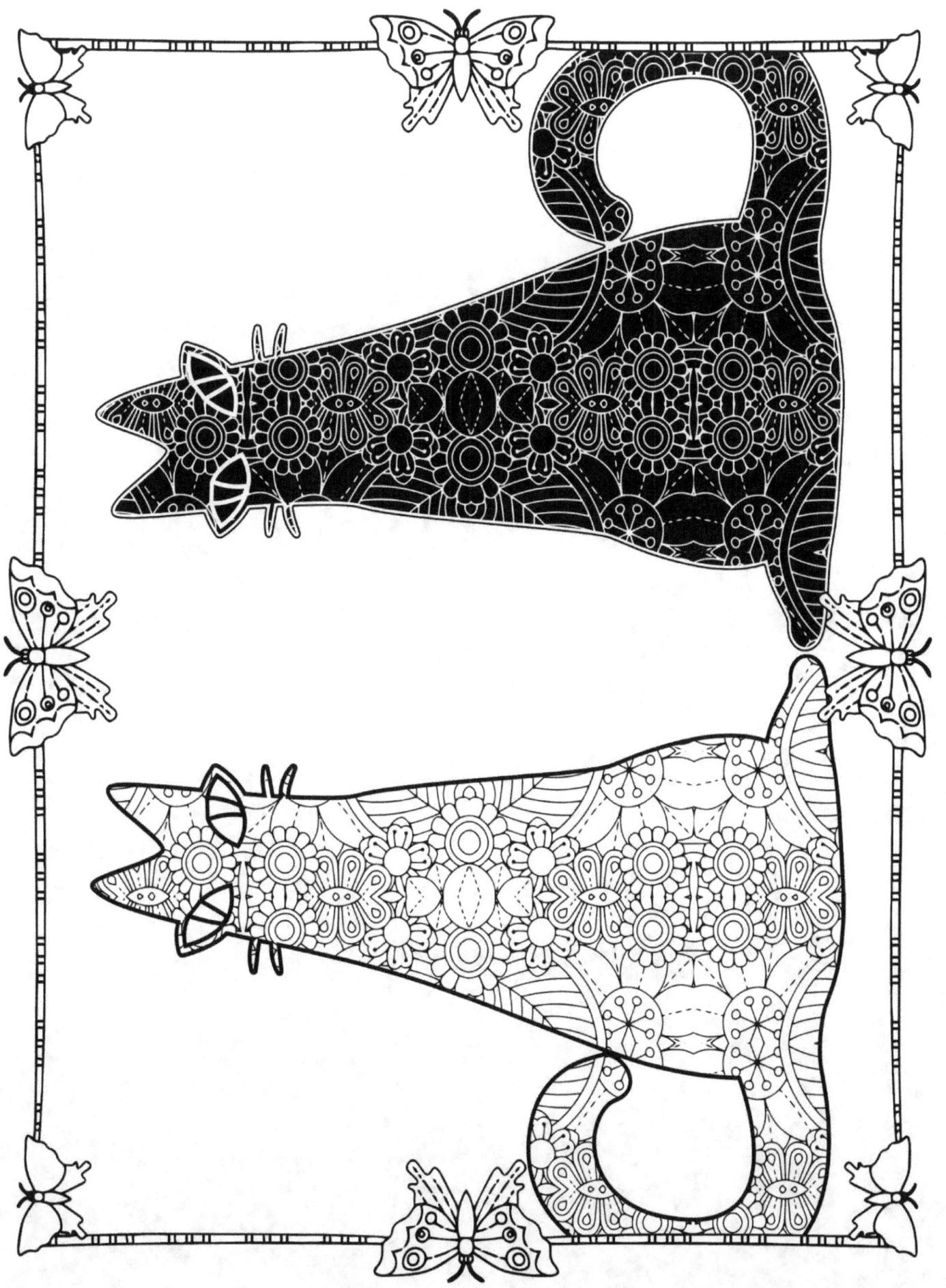

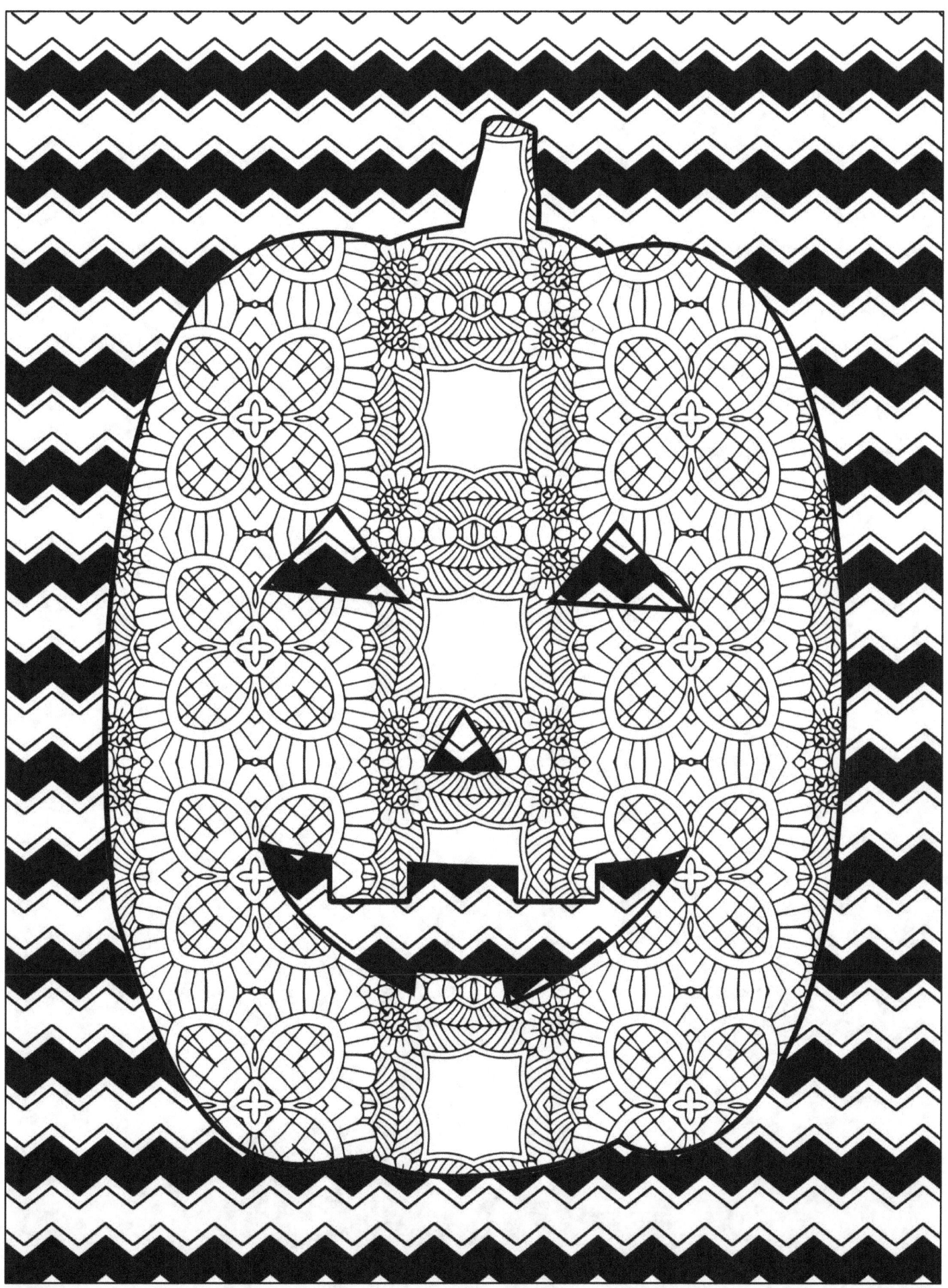

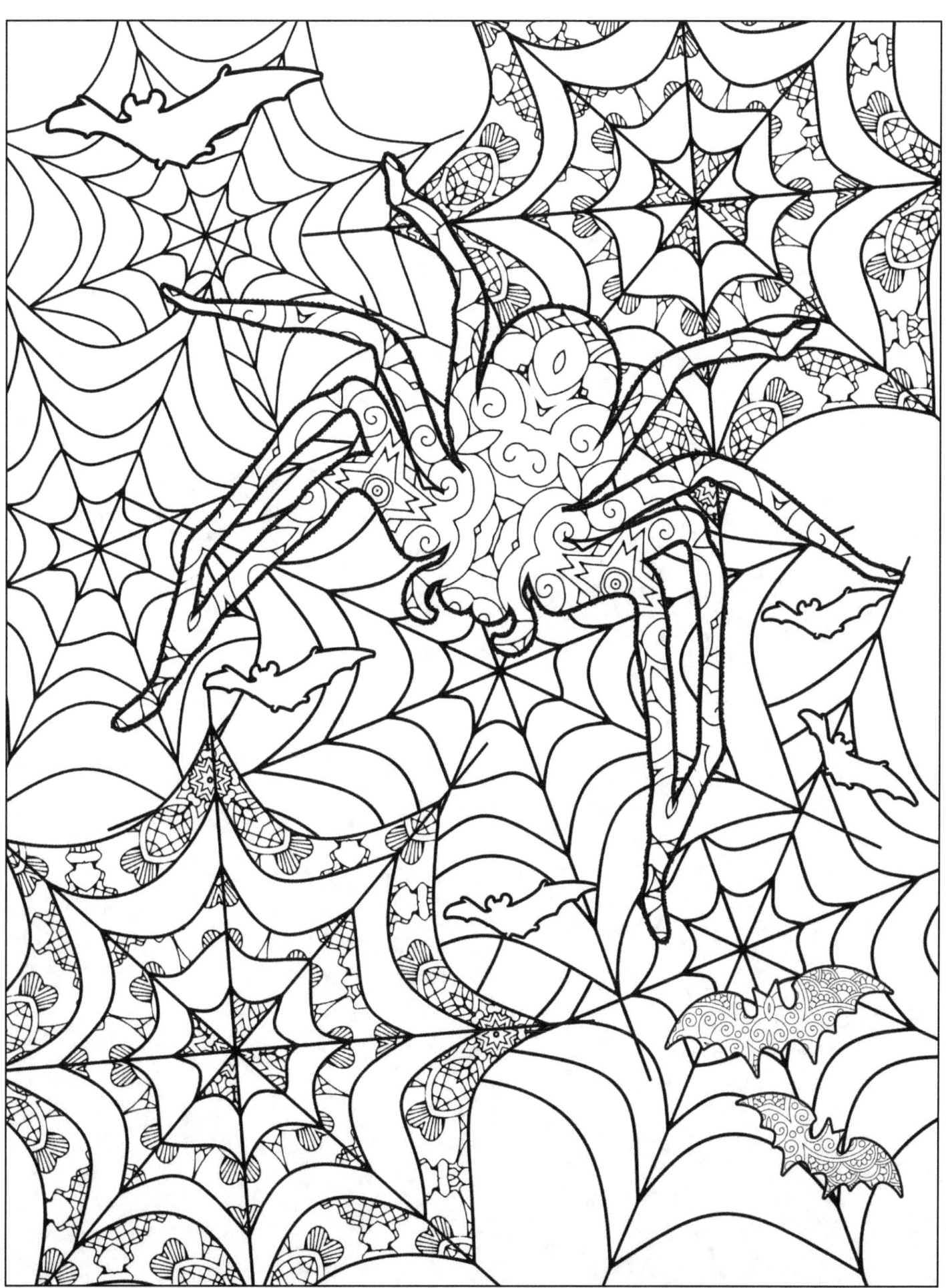

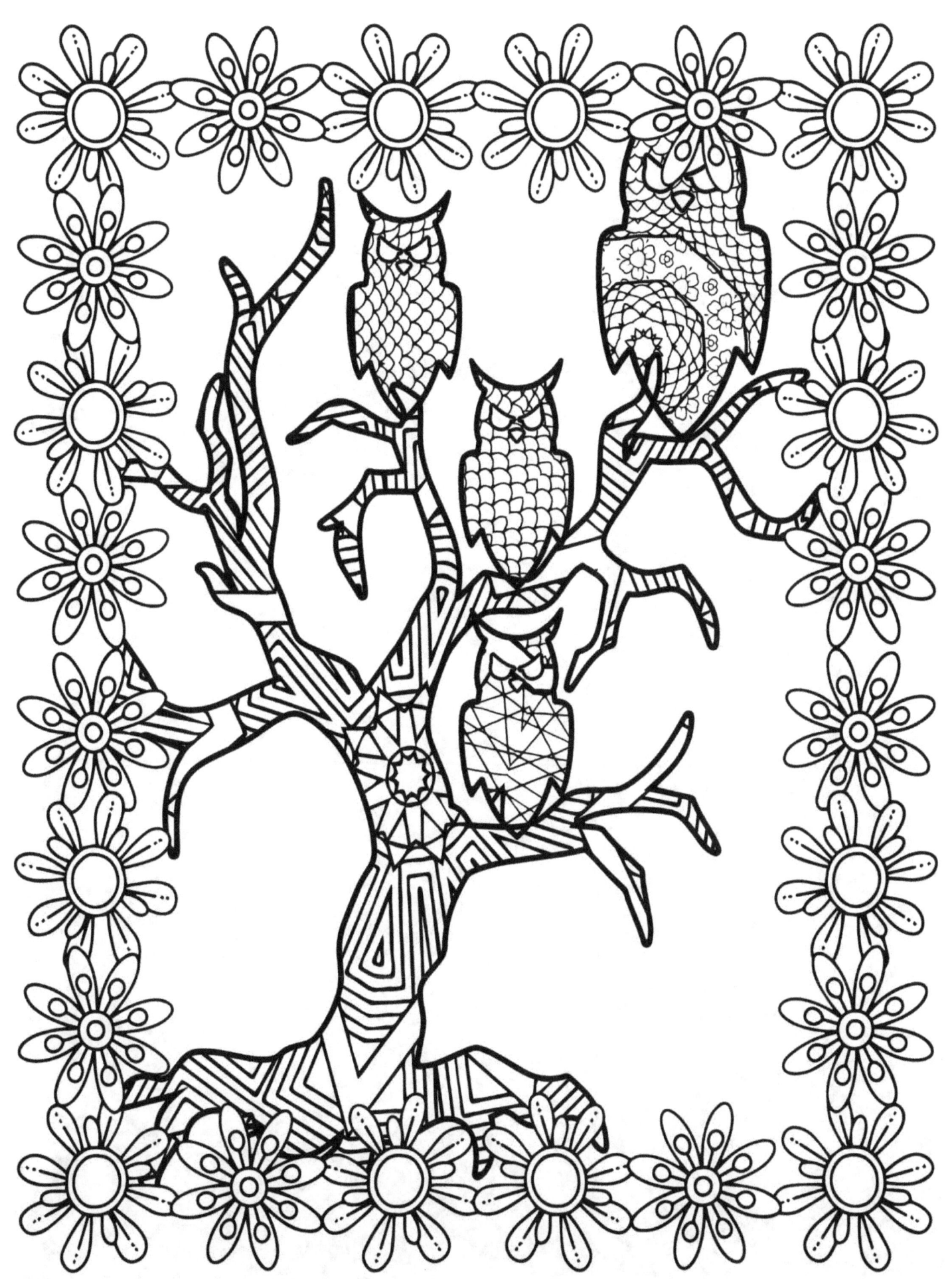

OTHER COLORING BOOKS BY NERINE MARTIN

Mandalas for Mindfulness Volume 1
Mandalas for Mindfulness Volume 2
Neon Mandalas for Mindfulness Volume 3
Mandalas for Mindfulness: Black & White Edition Volume 4
Patterns for Mindfulness: RELAX Volume 1
Color Your Way Through Anxiety
My Coloring Organizer
Color Your Way Around USA
Merry Christmas
Christmas
Happy Halloween
*Dashing Designs
*Angels and Crosses
*Trees and Reindeer
*Holiday Bulbs
*Holiday Stars
*Christmas Trees
*Christmas Stockings
*Christmas Ornaments
*Festive Phrases
*Ugly Sweaters
*Love Hearts
*Valentine Coloring Pages

You can also find Nerine's designs featured in:
Adult Coloring Book Treasury 1
Adult Coloring Book Treasury 2
(Available from Amazon)

*Only available as a PDF Version from www.ColorYourWayToHappy.com

Share your colored pages from Nerine's books at:
www.facebook.com/ColorYourWayToHappy

The *Color Your Way To Happy* adult coloring book series,
offers you an escape from the daily pressures of life,
to a relaxing state of calm and mindfulness.

Grab your copy today and go 'Color Your Way To Happy'.

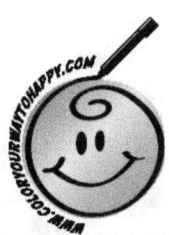

Tear out this blotter page and place behind
the page you are coloring to protect from bleed through ☺

Tear out this blotter page and place behind
the page you are coloring to protect from bleed through ☺

www.ingramcontent.com/pod-product-compliance
Lightning Source LLC
Chambersburg PA
CBHW081745220526
45468CB00008B/2243